D1706909

53 Essential Bug Out Bag Supplies

How to Build a Suburban "Go Bag" You Can Rely Upon

2nd Edition

by Damian Brindle

===> Get dozens of free survival guides, hundreds of videos, 600+ "how to" articles, gear reviews and so much more here: https://rethinksurvival.com

Disclaimer

Table of Contents

Introduction

This book is intended to provide useful, actionable survival strategies as quickly as possible. As such, it's written to be fast to read and includes minimal product images. Links are provided to referenced products should you want additional information or to purchase the product.

About Website Links

Realize, too, that this was originally written to be an electronic book only with many website links referenced throughout. Because this is a paperback book, however, referencing these links can be tedious if you had to type them into your web browser by hand. To make this easier on you, I have consolidated all referenced links into one page here: https://rethinksurvival.com/books/bag-links-2.html.

When new links are introduced, they will be referenced with superscripts which will then correspond to the appropriate URL on the above referenced website page.

For completeness, all referenced links will also be included in Appendix F.

Grab Your Free 53-Point Checklist

Odds are that you won't remember everything discussed when you're done reading this book. To make your life easier I've created a free, easy-to-reference 53-point bug out bag checklist that you can download, which outlines everything discussed herein. You'll find a link to it here so that you can follow along if you like as well as at the end of this book in Appendix A, but please do read the entire book first. Now, download your free, easy-to-reference bug out bag checklist here.[1]

Prepare Yourself for Natural Disaster in Only 5 Minutes

Since you clearly understand the need for safety, I want to share with you my unique **5 Minute Survival Blueprint** where you'll discover just how to keep your family safe and secure from disasters of all kinds in only 5 minutes a day quickly, easily and inexpensively.[2]

More Survival Books You'll Enjoy

If you liked what you read when finished, you can find more survival books I've written at https://rethinksurvival.com/kindle-books.[3]

This Book's Tone

As noted before, this book is written in a quick, simple, easy to read format. Hence, it is presented in a conversational form and not one that is intended to be grammatically correct. Getting YOU and your family ready for emergencies is the sole focus of this book.

And My Thanks...

I also want to thank those folks who took the time to review this book, to offer their own suggestions, and to correct my mistakes. You know who you are.

What Does Bug Out Mean?

Although the term is commonplace among preppers, you might not yet know what it means. Ultimately, to bug out means to evacuate your home should a disaster strike and force you to leave. While an evacuation can be done by car or on foot—and either scenario would necessitate having supplies with you—a bug out bag (also known as a *go bag*) typically refers to the bag of essential items you must take with you when evacuating by foot.

Being ready and able to bug out or evacuate from a disaster is no easy task and doing so on foot surely makes a bug out situation THAT much more difficult. Let us hope you never have to evacuate like this but, if you do, then you ought to get it right. Having your bug out bag gear correct is a great first step, a step which most people, even experts, get wrong.

Why Would I Need to Evacuate?

Most any disaster could force you to evacuate, from hurricanes and tornadoes to earthquakes and wildfires, to name a few. Of course, not every disaster scenario requires an evacuation, but many do. The folks who had to flee for their lives in the recent California wildfires would be a prime example. Those directly affected by floods in Texas and the Midwest in recent years found need to evacuate unexpectedly too. Hurricanes force unwanted evacuations year in and year out as Hurricanes Harvey and Irma made abundantly clear.

Be aware, too, that a bug out bag may be of use even after a disaster has struck since the aftermath could be equally terrible for your survival. For instance, imagine having just survived a massive earthquake where once recognizable buildings are now rubble and infrastructure is devastated. That would be no place to be for some time to come. The same could be said for a tornado that just ripped through your town. Surely it would make sense to even flee a disaster's aftermath to ensure you and your family stay safe.

Finally, understand that, although this book is intended to create a bug out bag for an on foot evacuation, there's no reason why you couldn't also take this bag during an evacuation in a vehicle. I happen to keep mine in my vehicle for this very reason. No matter what you choose to do, I would encourage you to already have some additional survival supplies in your vehicles just in case.

How Long Should I Plan For?

Most recommendations are to plan for two or three days and I see no reason to recommend anything beyond that, particularly since the purpose of this bug out bag is to get you out of harm's way and to a nearby town or city which was unaffected (or less affected) by the same disaster that caused you to flee in the first place.

Ideally, I would expect you to have a handful of locations to which you could walk within a day or two. As such, you will want to pack for two or three days which is one day longer than expected to give you a cushion in the event you're delayed or plans changed midway into your evacuation. If you'll have a longer walk than even a few days, then pack accordingly. And if that's the case then it's most likely you don't live in a very urban or suburban environment and, therefore, should pack a bug out bag tailored towards wilderness survival.

Now, if you wanted to pack enough supplies for a week or longer then you could certainly do so. Clothes and most of your gear should be useful for many days in a row. Some foods, especially freeze-dried foods if you choose them, take up relatively little space and weight too. The biggest problem you will likely have during an extended bug out is water procurement. Unfortunately, water may be difficult to come by in an urban or suburban evacuation seeing as though most of us are accustomed to simply turning on the nearest faucet.

How This List is Broken Down

Most checklists you'll find breakdown your bug out bag into obvious categories, such as water, food, clothing, first aid supplies, and so on. This makes intuitive sense, but I wanted to look at the topic a bit differently so that you can purchase gear as money permits because, let's face it, building a bug out bag from scratch isn't cheap.

To facilitate this, I've separated this list into four tiers of gear. Tier one gear is, in my opinion, the most likely to be used and to be useful by most folks during a suburban bug out. Tier two is a bit less likely to be used than tier one, tier three even less so, with tier four being the least potentially used in most cases. That said, don't underestimate the usefulness of tiers three and four gear, as they could be lifesavers in the right circumstance.

After I've finished with the list of 53 essentials, I'll also outline what I feel are unnecessary gear and supplies that many lists would normally include in a typical bug out bag. Personally, I wouldn't bother with any of the gear in this list unless you know of some specific reason why you should include it, such as a nearby fishing hole you expect to make use of.

The Assumptions I'm Making

So that you understand where I'm coming from, I want to be clear from the start:

- You're expected to get somewhere safe within a day or two, three days tops.
- You're bugging out into and through suburbia, NOT the wilderness.
- You want to haul less stuff, not more.

In addition, this bag is intended for one adult only. Duplicate it for other family members and adjust as needed for dependent children who cannot carry much of their own gear yet. In fact, if you have young children for whom you need to carry their gear then you're going to need a bigger backpack than the one I recommend shortly. Something that's 80-liters in capacity or larger is probably necessary.

Regrettably, most every bug out bag list has some unwritten expectation that you're going to be evacuating into or through a plentiful nearby wilderness with fish to catch, streams to rest alongside, mountains to navigate, and debris huts to build. This just isn't the case for most of us.

Most Americans are going to be slogging their way through the urban jungle with nothing to catch for food or even a good source of water to drink. There may even be potentially unrecognizable building and roads as well as a shortage of safe shelter spots to get out of the elements. There will even be unprepared and desperate people looking for any way to survive which could mean looking to YOU for whatever you may be able to provide, willingly or not.

These juxtapositions in bug out environments are quite different and should be treated as such. We, therefore, need to plan differently for a bug out in suburbia as opposed to the wilderness. Throw out old notions of stuffing your bag with fishing kits, hydration bladders, axes, saws, and tents.

Now, before we get into the specifics, we must discuss the elephant in the room when it comes to creating such a list.

The Problem with Creating an Ultimate Bug Out Bag List

My bug out bag cannot be your bug out bag. It just can't. We're different people, sometimes have different needs, probably live in different areas, likely have different skills, and may even have different expectations during a bug out.

Even so, as different as our bug out bags can invariably be there will, no doubt, be similarities upon which we can rely. Here is where we'll start our journey, that is, on common ground. Specifically, we'll consider the gear and supplies which I feel that most folks can reasonably assume they'll need during a suburban evacuation.

Personally, I've stopped trying to include anything and everything that I possibly can in my bag. It's just not a reasonable approach anymore. Instead, I've focused on these fifty-three essentials, and I feel you should as well.

Of course, if you have a need to add anything else not mentioned herein, feel free. Just focus on what I recommend before going overboard on anything else to ensure you're covered.

Boost Your Skills and Competence

What this book doesn't include are the skills and knowledge of how to use this gear properly and safely. One can have the best gear in the world and if you have no idea how to make use of it, largely gained through experience, it will do you little good. You could even harm yourself or others if you do something wrong due to ignorance.

Please take some time to understand how to use this gear properly, particularly first aid supplies, so that you will know what to do when the time comes. And, while YouTube videos will help, I would encourage you to find somebody you trust, maybe a friend or family member, who can teach you via hands-on application.

Choosing a Bag: Which Comes First, The Bag or The Gear?

There are two schools of thought here:

1. Choose your gear and then find an appropriately sized hiking bag to fit it all.
2. Find a hiking bag you like and then choose gear that will fit within the bag.

Both have their merits, though, the former threatens to weigh you down whereas the latter could leave you compromising on gear or, worse, without something essential because it just didn't quite fit in the bag you chose.

As I'm getting older, I've noticed that pack weight is more of a concern for me than ever before and I suspect it is for you too. If this is the case for you as well then choose the bag first and do your best to make the gear fit. Odds are that you'll be able to do so with a little creativity. I'll offer suggestions below, but you may have to adjust your gear a bit to make everything fit.

If, on the other hand, you're still a fit twenty-year-old and ready to take on the world then grab all the gear you like and find a bag that works to contain it all. Of course, be sure to consider pack weight, with the general rule of thumb being that your pack shouldn't weigh more than one-third of your body weight.

Realize, however, that whatever bag you choose should be a good quality hiking backpack with appropriate waist straps to transfer the bag's weight to your hips; your typical school backpack just won't do the job here, so please don't even try.

I recognize, too, that some folks just can't carry any sort of bag for long distances, especially for a lengthy evacuation on foot. There are a few alternatives which may work, such as a rolling suitcase or duffel bag, a garden wagon, or even a pull-behind stroller that attaches to a bicycle, to name a few examples.[4] Granted, these aren't ideal alternatives, but I'm hoping they will get you thinking outside of the box so to speak if a hiking backpack just won't work for you.

Moreover, a lot of the gear discussed is small. Consider using a few dry bags or other small stuff sacks to keep your gear contained, organized, and dry. If you prefer a lesser expensive option, sturdy gallon- or quart-sized plastic freezer bags will work well enough, though they're not recommended for long-term use. At the very least, plastic Ziploc bags can be used to further organize your supplies inside of an appropriate dry bag. There's also no harm with including a few unused gallon Ziploc bags for use as an expedient dry bag or to transfer water more easily.

Which Hiking Bag Should You Purchase?

Recommending a hiking backpack is difficult because the choice is so very personal and they're surprisingly different. For starters, there are external-frame, internal-frame, and even frameless backpacks. They come in many sizes (or load capacities), can be made from different materials, may have a variety of color choices, and definitely range in price. Some have many more pockets than you know what to do with, and still others have specialized straps or attachment points. As such, I would suggest you become more familiar with your backpack options before blindly accepting my specific recommendation below if you have no idea what to look for.[5]

I chose to purchase new bags because I wanted to downsize from the even larger 80-liter bags we had been using which were getting old and had a few problems that needed fixed.

With that in mind, I recently purchased two Nevo Rhino 50-liter Internal Frame Backpacks for our bug out bags since they were a good price and about the right size for us and our gear.[6] Although they didn't include the typical zippered side and front pockets that I was accustomed to, I was able to make it all work out and I believe you will too. Here's what they look like from the front and back:

And, while I was able to fit all of my gear and supply recommendations into the newer Nevo bags, it would be stretching things to make them useful for a bug out beyond two or three days. Plus, if you needed to include items like a sleeping bag or extra cold weather gear then you would probably want something larger. Even so, these bags do have straps on the outside to attach items like trekking poles or a sleeping pad.

Of course, there are better hiking backpacks out there if you're willing to spend the money. If you think you're going to also use these bags for occasional backpacking trips or you want something more rugged, invest in a better bag.

Tier 1 Items: Never Leave Home Without These

Following are the gear and supplies which are most likely to be used and to be found useful by the majority of folks during an evacuation. I strongly encourage you to add all the recommendations included here to your bug out bag since you're almost assured to make use of them or they're about the only option to ensure your safety, such as the water filter or first aid kit.

1. Bug Out Plan, Information

Evacuating with a lot of gear on your back will do you little good if you have no idea where you're headed or how to get there. That's what the unprepared masses will do. I hope you won't do that.

There's a lot of information you could include in your bug out plans, and if you want to know all of it, consider my 12 Pillars Of Survival program.[7] To be honest, though, there's really only three main pieces of information everyone should include: a checklist of gear and supplies, evacuation procedures, and emergency contacts.

While I discuss these documents in further detail later on in the chapters covering evacuation, I will say the following now:

- The checklist of gear and supplies lists those items you need to take with you during an evacuation by vehicle. This could include extra food, pet supplies, and camping gear, to name a few suggestions.
- The evacuation procedures will include details on where and when you'll evacuate, particularly routes to get there safely, whether by vehicle or by foot.
- The emergency contacts worksheet will include a wide variety of numbers you may want to have on hand after a disaster, such as to file an insurance claim, reputable recovery services, utility providers, healthcare providers or pharmacies, and more.

You can find these worksheets in PDF format for free here: https://rethinksurvival.com/books/plans.html.[8] If you'd prefer not to make use of my suggestions for whatever reason, then you can always write down your own evacuation plans by hand. The important part is to include multiple evacuation destinations, in different cardinal directions (north, south, east, and west), with two different routes to get there. Include maps with routes highlighted and even other details, such as rest stops or rendezvous points, and you'll be well ahead of almost everyone else.

Besides my tools and advice given later on, this guide will help you get the idea of how to plan your evacuation routes if you've never done so before.[9]

2. Change of Clothes, Shoes

Unless you can get to where you need to be within a few hours, and even if you can, you may find need to change clothes because they got soaking wet, for instance. It's also quite possible that the clothes you were wearing when you realized you needed to bug out are entirely wrong for the weather.

If possible, include an entire change of clothing from underclothes to outerwear. Avoid cotton clothes because they provide no insulating value when wet. Select at least lightweight pants and a long-sleeved shirt since each can be modified for warm weather (e.g., sleeves can be rolled up or completely cut off if you must) but a pair of shorts and a t-shirt just won't work for colder weather. You should also include an intermediate layer for additional warmth if you live in an area where it tends to get near or below freezing.

To save space, lay the clothes flat and roll together as tightly as possible. Now, secure them in place with something like a Velcro strap, cordage, or even several rubber bands if you must. Better yet, if you have a Foodsaver then place them in a Foodsaver bag and remove the air. This will better protect your clothes from the elements and help to save even more space.

Shoes are important as well. While I'd prefer you choose quality hiking boots, I understand not everyone has an extra pair of good boots lying around. At the very least toss in an old pair of sneakers that are still in decent shape as they will clearly be better than a pair of dress shoes, sandals, or nothing at all.

Finally, if you still have young kids at home, please be sure to check on and update their clothes and shoes at least twice a year. I know over the years that I was surprised at how quickly my boys would grow out of their clothes as well as their shoes and, honestly, I was lazy at times, not wanting to check on their supplies as often as I should have. If we'd had to evacuate, they might have not had what was needed. Check on their clothes and shoes at least once or twice a year.

3. Weatherproof Jacket, Rain Poncho

Being wet when you're forced to be out in the weather and on foot is a bad situation to find yourself in. You really need to ensure your core stays dry and a good weatherproof jacket is a great start. In fact, many jackets are so lightweight that they can be rolled up and squeezed into a small dry bag or Foodsaver bag and kept ready-to-go for years to come.

If you don't have a jacket to use, then your next best bet is a quality rain poncho. There are many to choose from but please don't buy those flimsy emergency or disposable rain ponchos that you can get for a dollar or two at places like your local department store, they're essentially garbage; you're almost better off, in fact, with an actual garbage bag as a makeshift poncho. Instead, get something more durable like this Frogg Togg's Ultra-Lite Poncho.[10] Because a rain poncho takes up so little space, I would encourage you to include more than one just in case you need to share with a family member.

4. Water Bottle, Canteen

Odds are fairly good that you'll need some water no matter what. Buy a good quality water bottle if you can. A stainless-steel bottle is preferred since they are more durable than their plastic counterparts and, more importantly, can be heated over a fire to boil or purify water, if need be. Something like this 40-ounce Klean Kanteen Wide-Mouth (Un-Painted) Water Bottle is what I have in mind.[11] Do NOT purchase a double-walled water bottle as they can explode if heated over a fire.

Whatever bottle you choose, get a slightly bigger bottle, let's say 27 ounces or more, so that you have a good amount of initial water with you. If you choose a 12-ounce bottle, for instance, you'd need to refill it at least twice as much as the 27-ounce option and three times as much as the 40-ounce bottle, which may not be possible during an evacuation.

The only drawback, of course, is the weight. Water is heavy and carrying a larger water bottle means more weight on your back which could be a concern if you can't handle heavy loads anymore, and even if you can.

While it's entirely up to you, you may want to fill the water bottle beforehand and stash it in your bag so that it's ready to go. So long as the bottle is clean and the water going in was clean then there should be no concern about the water going bad. If you do choose to do this then (1) leave a bit of headspace at the top of the bottle so water can expand if it freezes and (2) consider properly dosing the water with a drop or two of bleach (please do the math to get it right) to ensure the water stays potable. Here's a dosage reference if needed.[12]

Last, be sure to refill the bottle once or twice a year even if you've dosed the water with bleach to ensure it's as fresh as possible. If you're using a plastic bottle, then replace it once a year since plastics tend to leach chemicals into the water. And if you choose to include a hydration bladder, then leave it empty as the seams may burst if left filled and almost certainly if the bladder freezes, which could ruin your entire bug out bag and supplies.

5. Water Filtration Option

Many folks might choose a water purification options such as these Potable Aqua Tablets.[13] While an acceptable choice for a wilderness bug out—and there's really no harm with including them here, too—I'd prefer you get a water filter instead because you can drink water without any waiting and then get on the move again.

Though there are many other backpacking options, for the price, size, and effectiveness, you'd be hard-pressed to choose a better water filter than the LifeStraw Personal Water Filter.[14]

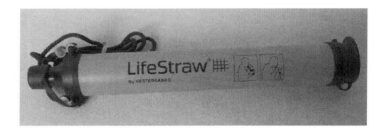

6. Quick Foods, Snacks, Hard Candies

Many bug out bags are geared towards meals, but not this one. You won't be cooking meals, nor should you. Instead, you're going to include foods that are quick snacks and can be eaten while on the go.

The reason is twofold: (1) you can live a few days without eating much—though my kids would disagree, and (2) you should be on the move as much as possible and stopping to cook meals could invite unwanted trouble.

Remember, bugging out in suburbia is NOT like bugging out into the wilderness! If people notice you cooking a hot meal while their stomachs are growling, you could be inviting unnecessary trouble which might otherwise have been avoided if you'd only kept a low profile and on the move.

Now, many shelf-stable foods could work here, but I'd suggest you opt for quick snacks such as granola bars, jerky, hard candies, and even these Datrex Emergency Food Bars or Mainstay Food Rations.[15, 16]

In my opinion, neither of the aforementioned food bars/rations taste great, but they'll last a long time and offer welcome nutrients as well as much-needed calories in a relatively small package.

Other foods to consider include tuna packets, protein powder, and even small canned foods with pop-top lids. If you search your local grocery store, you'll find plenty of small packaged foods that would be great for this purpose. Just be wary of adding too many canned foods because they will weigh you down. Here's an example of what I keep in my kids' bags, vacuum-sealed for longevity.

In the interest of being thorough, I'll mention that there's more food on the backside of the above photo which cannot be seen and may require utensils to eat, in particular, tuna packets, so be sure to include utensils as needed.

Also, be careful with adding foods that may appear shelf-stable yet can go rancid, such as some crackers, like Ritz, and nuts, specifically walnuts and pecans, as a few examples.

I should point out that if you intend to keep your bug out bag in a place where it's exposed to hot temperatures then you may not want to include any food at all since even the most stable of shelf-stable foods can and will eventually go bad in extreme temperatures and humidity.

Whatever foods you choose to include, please be sure to check on it a few times each year and replace it at least once each year regardless of where it's being stored, more often if it will be exposed to temperature or humidity extremes.

7. Flashlight, Headlamp

Flashlights are becoming so small, powerful, and efficient that there's no reason not to include one or two in your bag. I would prefer you get a quality flashlight such as this 2-AA Cell Maglite which is reasonably priced for its brightness and size.[17]

If you want a lesser expensive option, I've purchase several of these Cree Q5 LED Flashlights which work quite well for the price too and run on a single AA battery.[18]

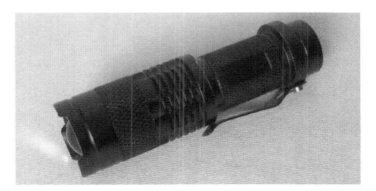

You can, in fact, get a pack of five of these flashlights for about the same price as the Maglite flashlight, but you may have to wait quite a while for them to ship from China depending on the vendor. At least, I had to for one of my orders. Of course, there are far better options than either of these flashlights if you're willing to spend the money as well as many other inexpensive options if you'll only look for them.

Regardless of the flashlight you opt for, be sure to include additional batteries. Check all batteries once or twice a year to ensure they didn't leak or otherwise go bad. If possible, don't keep the batteries installed in the event they leak and corrode your flashlight; this goes for all electronics that use batteries, by the way. That said, I would still choose to have one flashlight with the batteries already installed so that I have something to rely upon initially if it's dark out. This is another good reason to include two flashlights in your bag, one of which has batteries installed and is readily accessible.

I would also encourage you to purchase a headlamp in addition to a flashlight or two. Being able to have both hands free is awesome and especially useful during an emergency evacuation. At the very least, you won't have to carry a flashlight while walking.

Just as with flashlights, there are so many options and price-points for headlamps that it's mind boggling.

I've tried a few headlamps over the years with mixed results, but the technology keeps getting better and cheaper so I'm not going to offer a specific suggestion here. Somewhere around twenty dollars should land you a decent headlamp for sure.

Last, it never hurts to try and standardize equipment to use either AA or AAA batteries, but that's not always easy to do. Most headlamps, it seems, tend to use AAA batteries and, so, it could be useful to purchase flashlights that also use AAA batteries unlike the ones I recommend. Personally, I don't see this as a huge issue since other battery-powered equipment I recommend use a mix of either AA or AAA batteries. Do your best to avoid oddball battery sizes and you'll be fine.

8. Local Maps

While a GPS is useful during everyday life, it may not function during an emergency. Just buy an appropriate local map from Walmart and keep it sealed in something like a Ziploc bag for a bit of water protection, or use a trusty Foodsaver bag, if you prefer.

You probably only need one local area map and nothing more, but if there's something unique to your situation, such as living at the edge of a map zone, then get whatever you need. State maps probably aren't necessary for a bug out on foot, neither is a road atlas. That said, you may want more detailed local maps of your chosen long-distance bug out destinations which you'll have to purchase online.

Alternatively, consider utilizing the offline maps app I discuss in my book *27 Crucial Smartphone Apps for Survival* as a backup resource or even in place of purchasing out-of-area maps.[19] It's what I do. I realize that this is potentially risky because phones can get damaged, lost, or run out of batteries, but I consider it an acceptable risk because it's my local area which is the danger area, and I already have a paper map to cover that.

9. Self-Defense Options

I know this doesn't seem like something you WILL make use of, after all, the odds of having a serious, even life-threatening, physical confrontation during an evacuation seems far-fetched. Plus, it's not like we hear about people being attacked during natural disasters left and right. It does happen, but not as a matter of course.

That said, if there is a time where you're more likely to be a target of somebody's rage and fear, it's when you're vulnerable, when people are stressed, when situations are in flux, and a disaster brings these elements together like nothing else. With that in mind, I would encourage you to have the ability to protect yourself and your loved ones should a confrontation occur.

How you handle this is totally your call, but whether you include a self-defense option directly in your bug out bag or as part of your everyday carry, you should seriously consider adding something.

The obvious options include firearms, knives, pepper spray, and tasers. Less obvious options include a small baseball bat, lead pipe, kubotan, brass knuckles, self-defense key chain rings, as well as a variety of makeshift weapons I won't attempt to mention here. As another example, I also keep a collapsible baton in my bag as a backup option.

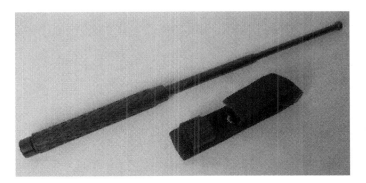

Whatever you choose, be sure to follow all local and state laws regarding your choices as some options are illegal everywhere. Also, be aware that the theft of a firearm, in particular, could pose a potential legal problem for you down the road. Finally, be aware that children may gain access to a weapon in your bug out bag as well. Just be careful and safe with your choice here.

10. Portable Phone Charger, Extra Cords

Nearly all of us rely on our phones these days and if you've read my smartphone survival apps book then you realize just how important a smartphone can be to your survival during an emergency.

As such, I would strongly encourage you to have the ability to keep it charged and functioning for as long as possible. Besides having a charging block and additional cords appropriate to your phone, which can often be found online for a few dollars each, I would also suggest that you purchase a portable USB charger.

Personally, I've purchased several different chargers over the years, some better than others. And just as with headlamps, the storage capacity, relative size, and price keep changing drastically as technology gets better, so I'm hesitant to offer a specific suggestion. In any case, I recently bought two Beston10,000mAh Portable Chargers for under ten dollars each for our bug out bags.[20]

11. Pocket Radio

Any AM/FM pocket radio should work well here, and if it includes shortwave bands or NOAA weather alerts then that's a bonus. As you might suspect, the better pocket radios are a bit expensive. Even so, I've found that you can easily find a decent option for around $20, such as this Tecsun AM/FM/Shortwave Compact Radio.[21]

While I'm thinking about it, you should know what your local radio emergency broadcast stations are.[22] When you find yours go write it down if you can't remember the station; directly on the inside of the battery cover works, that way you'll never lose it.

I should point out that there are AM/FM radio apps for your smartphone which you may be tempted to use in place of an actual radio. It's tempting because, so long as you have a pair of headphones or earbuds plugged in to act as the antenna, these apps should be able to pick up radio stations from almost anywhere. The problem, however, is that you must have an internet connection to get them to work which isn't a sure thing during a disaster.

Instead, keep a small pocket radio in your bag and you're sure to have access to your local emergency radio stations.

12. Cash, Small Bills

You might need cash during an evacuation for any number of reasons. For instance, you might need to purchase sundries, gasoline, rent a hotel room, or buy your way out of a sticky situation. Who knows what else you might need to pay for that you didn't expect?

I do know for sure that cash will continue to be accepted by nearly everyone in almost any circumstance. Realize, too, that debit and credit cards probably won't work and that checks likely won't be accepted either because they cannot be verified electronically. Therefore, cash is the only reliable currency during a disaster.

How much to keep in your bag? Obviously, that's up to you, but I wouldn't suggest adding thousands of dollars in the event your bag gets stolen. A few hundred dollars, on the other hand, should be enough to be useful. If you can't afford that much, then even a few twenty-dollar bills is better than nothing. It couldn't hurt to distribute some cash to different spots on your body and among group members.

Moreover, I wouldn't suggest you include any pocket change as it will just weight you down and be of little use. Similarly, including precious metals would be a waste here as well since most people wouldn't even know what you're handing them. Last, include small bills, nothing larger than twenties, in the event other people just can't make change and maybe some five-dollar bills for a vending machine.

13. Ultralight Tarp

Why include a tarp? Besides keeping the rain off you and your gear, a tarp can be used to provide shade, as a windbreak, ground cover, and even to collect rainwater, to name a few possible uses. As such, there's no reason not to include one in your bag.

Besides the aforementioned uses, an ultralight tarp like the one I will suggest can be packed down to almost nothing and can be easily configured in a variety of ways to aid with your overall comfort and survival.

Could you use a typical rip-stop tarp instead of an ultralight tarp? Sure, you can. Just be aware that it will be heavier and won't pack down nearly as well as an ultralight option.

Regardless of the covering you opt for, the two biggest drawbacks with including any tarp are that (1) there could be very few structures from which to attach a tarp and (2) most quality ultralight tarps are a bit expensive for what seems like little in return.

No doubt, the likelihood of NOT having a good standing structure or even a few trees from which to string up a tarp in a suburban bug out is a legitimate concern. If this were a wilderness situation, then I would say that choosing a tarp is an easy decision since there will clearly be plenty of trees to make use of. Regardless, any large covering can be invaluable in a survival situation even if it cannot be strung up since it can still be used as additional protection from the rain or wind, even if it's only draped over you.

In addition, a quality ultralight tarp could serve you well for many years if you do any sort of camping or backpacking whatsoever. Even if it's only for your bug out bag, though, an ultralight tarp may be a welcome addition simply to save on weight and space.

What about opting for a tent instead? Personally, I prefer tarps to tents for evacuation purposes simply because they take up less space in your bag and can be configured differently than a tent. That said, I can see how some folks may prefer a tent, for instance, if you have small children who would feel safer in a tent.

Realize that there are many lightweight tarp options available but, if you need a suggestion, try this Aqua Quest Glide Sil Tarp as a quality option.[23]

Finally, if you're going to include a tarp then you're going to want some cordage with which to string it up. You may also want stakes to hold things down and maybe even guyline tensioners, neither of which are expensive, yet tend to make setup easier.

14. First Aid Supplies

Accidents happen, even after a disaster. With that in mind, the most likely first aid concerns after a disaster would probably be cuts and lacerations, burns, and maybe even sprains and strains. Concussions may also be a concern as well.

To ensure you're covered for the minimum of troubles, include basic first aid supplies such as bandages, especially knuckle and finger bandages, non-stick gauze and even gauze rolls, non-latex gloves, a triangular bandage or two, antibiotic ointment, moleskin for protecting blisters, burn cream, eye drops or a small bottle of eye wash solution, and maybe something for dental pain or a temporary dental filling. Medications will be discussed next.

Personally, I like to vacuum-seal my supplies to ensure they stay dry, but even a Ziploc bag is better than nothing.

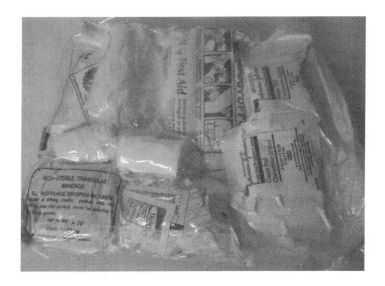

You don't need to go overboard here. Just ensure you have the basics so that you can deal with small first aid concerns like those I mentioned previously.

From my experience, I would suggest you assemble your own small first aid kit rather than to buy anything which comes pre-packaged. Most of the time these pre-packaged kits sound great yet seem to include hundreds of bandages you'll never use and little else. Instead, choose to assemble your own mini first aid kit to ensure you get it right. And if you have more than one bug out bag to assemble then assembling your own kits will be that much more cost-effective.

15. OTC Medications / Prescription Pills

Medications are another big item to consider, but you likely won't need to include a wide variety of over-the-counter medications.

Regardless, if you have prescription pills that you take regularly then be sure to include a minimum of several days' worth (two weeks is better) assuming, of course, that they're shelf-stable. **If you take life-necessary prescription medications, then I would encourage you to have thirty days' worth of pills or more**. Most doctors should support this. If not, consider finding a new doctor.

You really shouldn't shortchange yourself here because you never know what the situation may be like wherever it is that you end up. That is, you may not be able to get the pills which you need immediately upon arrival, then what will you do? Don't let this happen to you.

Besides any prescription medications you may need, add some Ibuprofen and Tylenol for pain relief, Benadryl pills which is an antihistamine, electrolytes to keep your salt and sugars in balance, as well as an anti-diarrheal and anti-constipation meds to round things out.

You may be wondering why you would want to include the anti-diarrheal and anti-constipation medications. The answer is that evacuations tend to bring stress and stress tends to bring digestive problems. These pills are meant to help alleviate short-term bowel issues should they arise. Plus, if you're eating MREs then you could exacerbate bowel troubles.

Include any child-specific medications as well. I'd strongly prefer they were NOT liquid medications since these tend to go bad much faster than solid medications and could potentially leak thereby ruining your gear as well. That said, you shouldn't assume a child can take adult medications even if cut in half, so be sure to include appropriate shelf-stable medications for children, if you think you'll need them.

What if Your Medications are Liquid or Need to be Refrigerated?

If it's liquid and shelf-stable, then I would double- or triple-bag the medication in quality Ziploc bags or use a Foodsaver for a better airtight seal. If it needs to be refrigerated, then consider some sort of mini cooler travel bag, such as these Travel Cooler Bags which are made for insulin.[24] They're not perfect, but it's better than your medications getting warm. That said, talk to your doctor or pharmacist just in case your medications shouldn't freeze as well as what problems may arise if they get too warm.

Finally, you're going to want to replace all medications on a regular basis. I don't know what that is for your prescription medications, but for over-the-counter pills I would check on them once a year just to be sure they didn't clearly disintegrate due to humidity and, at the very least, replace all medications before their expiration date.

16. Extra Glasses, Contacts, Hearing Aid Batteries, etc.

Whatever you need to keep your faculties in order and body able to function, add it to your bag now, specifically glasses, contacts, hearing aid batteries, false teeth or other dental needs, assorted back or knee braces, and so on. If you need these items to function, then they should be at the top of your list.

Tier 2 Items: Gear to Make Your Evacuation Easier

These recommendations are slightly less likely to be used or to be found useful than tier one gear yet shouldn't be ignored as they can make your evacuation easier, even pleasant, in a variety of suburban bug out situations. I encourage you to include them.

17. Hat, Bandanna

Being able to keep the sun or rain off your face and head will increase your comfort level ten-fold. Now, while any old ball cap will do just that, a wide brim hat is usually a better choice for full coverage of your neck as well. Plus, they can easily be rolled up to save space without ruining the hat.

Bandannas, too, have dozens of potential survival uses, from a makeshift sling to a face mask or neck cover, you name it, a bandanna can probably do it. Since they're relatively inexpensive and lightweight, include more than one in your bag.

Try to purchase bandannas with heavier fabric rather than the flimsy cotton choices often found at local department stores because the flimsier ones usually won't stand up to much abuse. These bandannas look like what I've purchased before.[25]

18. Compass

You might be wondering why a compass is needed considering that you're not only bugging out in a town with street signs and roads, but also with a map in hand. There are few reasons, so let's tackle them one by one.

First, you may simply decide to go off the beaten path and, hence, find need to navigate without aid of signs and traditional roadways. In fact, this may be more likely than you realize considering that the shortest distance between two places is a straight line and following city streets typically doesn't wind up being the shortest pathway possible. As such, you may simply choose to bypass streets altogether where possible, and a compass will help you do just that.

Second, you could encounter downed or missing road signs, buildings damaged beyond recognition, and even entire areas that you were formerly accustomed to seeing which are now completely unrecognizable. How bad depends, of course, on the type of disaster that hit as well as to the extent of damage which could be far worse than most people realize. Just ask the folks who were devastated by the flooding in Japan if their towns were recognizable afterwards.

Third, you may simply be evacuating at night during which time familiar landmarks are less visible and, of course, there's no sun in the sky to aid you either.

Furthermore, if the power is out then you'll have an even more difficult time seeing anything that you may have relied upon to tell you where you are or where you're going.

Ultimately, you may only have a general idea as to which direction you need to go and, as such, a compass may help you find your way. You don't need anything special here. Just purchase a relatively decent compass online and you should be fine unless, of course, you plan on using a compass and map to orient yourself, in which case you'll want an orienteering compass.

19. Work Gloves / Nitrile Gloves

You never know what you may need to grip, grab, move, or touch during an evacuation. Do yourself a favor and buy a pair of good quality, form-fitting work gloves such as these Handyman Flex Grip Work Gloves and your hands will thank you.[26] Be aware that the link here is for the large gloves, though you can select another size if desired.

Additionally, considering that everything around you may be dirty at the very least, and possibly disease-ridden at worst, I might also suggest you include several pair of disposable nitrile gloves as an extra layer of protection. Plus, they're great for first aid uses too.

20. AMK Heatsheets / Bivvy

The clothes you're wearing, even the ones that you packed in your bag, may not be quite enough to keep you safe in bad weather. In fact, being exposed to the wind in chilly weather will drain your core body temperature fast and being wet will do so much faster. If you're unlucky enough to be both wet and in the wind, then you're in serious trouble.

Sadly, not all emergency blankets are made the same. Case in point, you've seen those flimsy emergency Mylar blankets, haven't you? You know, the ones that marathon runners are often seen draped with after a long run, the ones that are impossible to fold back into their original shape once unfolded? Yeah, those! They're horrible. Please get something better. This SOL Emergency Blanket is a better choice.[27]

If you prefer a two-person version, which might be a better choice even if it's just for you, then get this AMK Heatsheets Blanket.[28] Or, if you'd rather having something to crawl into like you would a sleeping bag, purchase the Go Time Gear Life Bivvy.[29]

In my opinion, the bivvy is the way to go since you can completely seal out the elements, but don't expect to be cozy and warm in cold weather because it's not a sleeping bag with inches of fluffy insulation. For the size and weight, though, it's hard to beat as an emergency single-person shelter.

21. MREs (not freeze-dried meals)

As much as I don't recommend MREs (Meals Ready to Eat or, formerly, K-Rations) for at-home preparedness, a bug out may be about the only time they're acceptable to me. Like I said previously, the goal in a suburban bug out isn't to fill your belly with a warm meal three times a day. As such, I prefer you just focus on including a variety of snacks and quick to consume foods if you simply must have something to eat.

That said, some folks may want a meal regardless of what I say. If you're one of them, then go with a few MREs instead of freeze-dried meals because MREs don't need boiling water to cook but, instead, usually include a handy heater which simply needs a bit of water to work.

You can either purchase entire meals or just the entrees. My suggestion is to go find a local Army surplus store or something similar, even some sporting goods stores sell them, and buy a few MRE meals or entrees that sound tasty, then take them home and try each one. Personally, I've found that about every other MRE entrée which I've tried isn't too bad.

Once you've found a few meals that you like buy them again and include these in your bag, but don't go overboard adding dozens of meals since you won't have room for anything else; two or three MREs will suffice. Last, MREs tend to make most people constipated when eaten regularly because they are very calorie dense. You have been warned.

22. Spork

I almost didn't bother to include eating utensils in this list at all because you're probably not going to be eating meals which require them. That said, I realize there could be some foods, such as canned fruit or packaged tuna and even some MRE entrees, which may necessitate a fork or spoon. And because we've already discussed food multiple times, including an eating utensil is appropriate now. This Light My Fire Spork is a good choice for the price and since there are four in a package you can include more than one in each bag or dole them out among bags.[30]

23. Binoculars / Monocular

As I mentioned a moment ago, the area you're traversing could be severely damaged, so much so that it's unrecognizable to you. You could, therefore, need to look ahead to where you're going or possibly to scout a better route around obstacles and debris. Or maybe the route ahead looks potentially dangerous for one reason or another. Being able to see what's coming before you get to it is a huge plus.

You don't need anything fancy here since most any pair of compact, folding binoculars will suffice for this purpose, such as these 8x21 magnification binoculars which are similar to what I have.[31]

If you want to save on weight and a bit of space, then a monocular may be the better choice. Also, if you think that you can use your cell phone camera zoom function or any magnifying glass app for this purpose, you can't, I've tried.

24. Sunblock

Sunburns hurt, and there's no reason for you or anyone else in your family to get one during a hasty evacuation either. Besides having appropriate clothing and a wide brim hat as I pointed out earlier, go buy a small tube or stick of sunblock of whatever brand you prefer.

As for what SPF to use, that's up to you. I would suggest something around SPF 30 to SPF 45 as it seems that anything outside of this range either isn't enough protection or overkill. Also, they make handy camping-style sunblock sticks which are around an ounce or less that would be perfect for this type of situation.

25. Insect Repellent / Mosquito Head Net

Just as with a sunburn, insects can get annoying, and when you're already stressed out the last thing you want to deal with are bugs pestering you. Get a small stick of insect repellent, something around one ounce or less, also often found in the camping section of your local department store, and you should be good to go. An alternative, if you'd prefer to avoid harsh chemicals, would be a mosquito head net which should keep all but the smallest of bugs at bay.

Wearing long-sleeved shirts and pants will go a long way toward keeping the bugs from bothering you too much as well. And if you live anywhere that insects are a real problem, then I would include both a mosquito head net along with more repellent.

26. Multi-tool

You never quite know why you might need a specific tool, but it's hard to do much if you don't have the appropriate one available, that's for sure. Even a simple screwdriver can be a lifesaver in the right situation. That said, who wants to carry around a small toolkit in their bag? Nobody, that's for sure.

This is why a trusty multi-tool is the perfect solution. Unfortunately, there are many choices, with each multi-tool offering a different set of tools, some drastically different, others not so much.

I've owned a Leatherman Wave for years and, while I love having it, there are multi-tools out there which may prove more useful to you and your situation, so it couldn't hurt to browse a bit. Regardless, the Leatherman Wave is my choice for a good quality pocket tool if you have no experience with them.[32]

27. FRS/GMRS Radios

While I assume you expect to stick together with your family throughout the entire journey, that may not be the case throughout the entire trip. For example, perhaps somebody will need to scout ahead or take a diversion to find a better route, shelter, or more supplies. Whatever the reason, I would encourage you to always stay in contact with them, and a trusty FRS/GMRS radio will help you do just that.

You don't need to spend a ton of money here but do get something that has the capability to use typical alkaline batteries rather than odd battery sizes or, worse, a proprietary rechargeable battery that cannot be replaced. Even these Motorola Talkabout Radios would be an acceptable choice, but really any handheld radios should work fine.[33]

Realize that handheld radios such as these probably won't transmit for long distances in a typical suburban environment due to buildings and other obstructions which will block the signal. Expect a half-mile or slightly more at the most.

Also, some handheld radios can use up batteries fast. As such, I would definitely include a spare set of batteries for each radio.

28. Hygiene Supplies

There's nothing like feeling normal when things are abnormal and being able to perform even basic hygiene tasks could make all the difference in your stress levels as well as for your general comfort. Even though you may not need to brush your teeth or comb your hair for a few days, which is why hygiene supplies were not considered until now, such items will surely be welcome and may even be in short supply wherever it is that you end up.

Include items like a travel toothbrush, toothpaste, floss, a small comb, pocket tissues, deodorant, and even lotion would be good too. I would add a travel-size bottle of hand sanitizer and liquid hand soap as well. Ladies will also want to include several feminine pads. I probably wouldn't bother with including shaving supplies or shampoo, but that's up to you. Just go visit the travel section of your local department store and you'll find what you need.

Also, because some of these supplies are liquid and could, therefore, ruin your other gear, be sure to package them appropriately in a Foodsaver bag or in Ziploc bags.

29. Wet Wipes / Toilet Paper

Although you should already have hand sanitizer and liquid soap as noted previously, I'd suggest you also include a small package of wet wipes since they're quick and easy to use while on the go. You should also include a half roll of toilet paper as well, packaged somehow to keep it from getting ruined if your bag gets wet.

30. Trauma Dressings

We've covered the basic first aid kit already. Regrettably, disasters are precisely the time where you could wind up with more than just a paper cut. Therefore, you're going to want something bigger and better than a bandage to cover a gaping wound, and an Israeli Compression Bandage will do just that.[34]

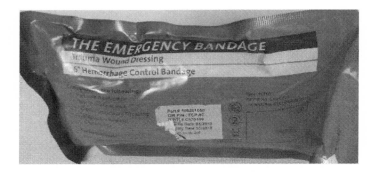

You may also choose to include a tourniquet as well as a few other serious first aid supplies. If this interests you, then you really need appropriate training. Also, watch this video for what to include as detailed by a prepper paramedic who offers sound advice for dealing with disaster first aid scenarios.[35]

31. Cordage, Wire Ties, or Straps

If you're going to include a tarp of any kind, then some cordage will be necessary. I see little reason to need more than a hundred feet. The typical go-to choice for bug out bag cordage is 550-paracord. Don't bother with anything fancy or expensive for your bug out bag since it's likely overkill, but if you simply must have something more durable, then try this X-Cords, 8-Strand Paracord.[36]

You might consider adding a Spool Tool which is a neat way to store and make use of paracord, though it's not necessary for your bug out bag.[37]

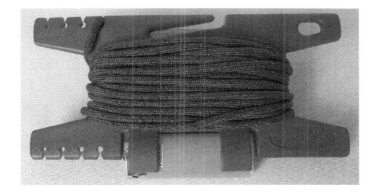

Wire ties or zip ties tend to be useful as well and, so, it couldn't hurt to include several medium sized ones—about eight to twelve inches in length—to your bag.

Another option would be to include a handful of hammock straps since they can be strung up and adjusted rather quickly, plus they are very strong. Honestly, though, if you can tie a few different styles of knots then you'll be fine with paracord alone.

Tier 3 Items: Not to Be Overlooked Situational Gear

My recommendations here also shouldn't be glossed over simply because they're not tier one or two inclusions. They're listed as tier three items only because the situation in which they're found useful may not happen to you. Please consider adding these items every bit as much as what's already been covered as money and time permit.

32. Fixed-Blade Knife

Unbelievably, I almost didn't include a knife here in tier three either and I can hear a few folks having a heart attack right now because of it. If this were a wilderness bug out then, yes, a quality fixed-blade knife would have been at the top of the list, but during a suburban bug out, not so much.

After all, it's not like you're going to be gutting a fish, gathering firewood, fashioning a spear, or building a debris hut in suburbia. A knife just isn't as important here and, so, there's little need for one. Granted, a knife can still be useful if for nothing more than as a potential self-defense option, though, firearms are the preferred choice.

What Knife Should You Buy?

As with some of my previous recommendations, there are so many options out there that you really need to get your hands on many different options to see what feels good to you. I can say this: don't go buying a packaged ten-dollar off-the-shelf knife or anything with a television celebrity's name on it, for that matter, as these usually aren't something to bet your life on.

That said, if you're going to get a knife then please do spend the money and get a good quality one, such as this Cold Steel Tanto.[38]

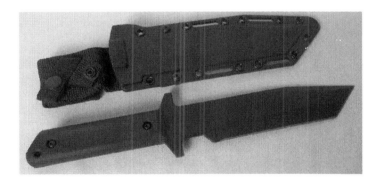

Truth be told that Cold Steel knife is a beast and more useful for wilderness survival. You're better off with something like this Gerber Gator fixed blade knife as a smaller, easier to use option.[39]

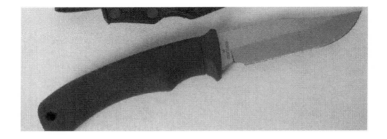

Last, a quality pocket folding knife may be the best alternative of them all in this situation, and if you carry one as part of your everyday carry gear like I do, then you'll be sure to always have a knife with you no matter what. Plus, foodsaver bags can be hard to open without a knife, which makes a small knife good to include.

33. Notepad and Pencil

Imagine that it's pouring rain and every time you try to jot down a few notes or maybe read what you wrote earlier, your notepad gets soaked. This can become frustrating rather quickly.

Now, while any small notepad and pencil or pen will do for jotting down quick notes when it's dry out, you have very few choices that will work in the rain. With this in mind, consider the Rite in the Rain Notebook, which is perfect for foul weather conditions and even if you accidentally drop your notepad in a puddle.[40]

You may want the accompanying Rite in the Rain All-Weather Pen to go with it or even a waterproof sharpie, though, a simple pencil works well enough most of the time.[41]

Of course, you may not need such specialized notetaking supplies whatsoever. After all, people have figured out how to shelter themselves and their supplies from the rain with a little ingenuity for a long time and I'm sure you can as well. Besides, smartphones make for useful notetaking devices as well so long as the batteries don't die.

34. Collapsible Water Bottle

Although you already have a water bottle, who knows what may happen to it. For example, the bottle could get cracked or otherwise damaged, you may lose it, or maybe you just don't want to share because of your fear of getting sick. A collapsible water bottle solves these problems and, while you could choose a smaller option, this one liter Vapur Water Bottle is a good choice.[42]

35. Whistle

Whistles are traditionally used for wilderness expeditions as a means of not only signaling for help but for communication between party members as well. The same can be done with suburban evacuations too. Each person should have their own whistle, so purchase as many as you need for your family now. Also, ensure the whistle you choose is a pea-less design so that it will work in freezing temperatures. I like the SOL Rescue Howler. Attach it to a length of quality paracord for easy access around your neck.[43]

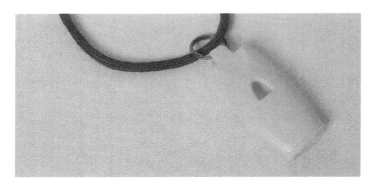

36. Fire Starters, Tinder

A Bic lighter, a box of strike anywhere matches, and a firesteel are all good to have just in case you need to start a fire for some reason. You can get the lighter and matches almost anywhere, but a quality firesteel is a bit more difficult to get locally sometimes, so I would suggest the Light My Fire Swedish Firesteel, also wrapped around a length of paracord with a whistle attached.[44]

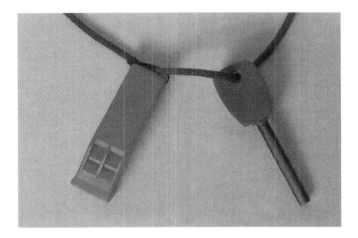

Include a bit of tinder as well. A few cotton balls or dryer lint will work, or you could buy some ready-made Tinder-Quik meant for camping or bug out applications.[45]

Like I said before, this isn't a typical wilderness evacuation and, therefore, you may not have to light a single fire. That said, it's darn hard to make a fire without the proper tools. And, because these items are so small and lightweight, there's no reason not to include them.

Also, if you're not familiar with a firesteel, then just skip adding one and include a few Bic lighters instead; you'll just be frustrated tying to use one. Similarly, matches sometimes don't work after years of storage either. Bic lighters, on the other hand, seem to be viable for a long time and quite durable.

37. N95 Masks

Remember 9-11? I'll bet you do. One of the scenes I remember most—besides the towers falling—was all the dust floating in the air. I remember seeing people running and trying to cover their nose and mouth with whatever they could. The problem is that most of their efforts did little good.

If they had a face mask they would have fared better. In fact, masks are not only useful for filtering out dust, but smoke and ash to a lesser extent as well. I'll bet some of those people who fled the California wildfires would have loved to have one too. Here's a PDF reference on the topic of wildfire smoke and face masks, if interested.[46]

Realize that an N-95 mask is typically the go-to option here. I must say, however, that they are (1) not easy to breathe with and (2) not 100% effective. That is, after all, the meaning behind the 95 aspect of the rating: they're 95% effective IF worn correctly, which still leaves at least 5% exposure.

To combat the first problem, you can purchase an N-95 mask with an exhalation valve, though, they're a bit more expensive than those without. Trust me when I say that you won't want to wear these masks for long regardless and that the exhalation valve merely makes them tolerable. Fortunately, you can buy N-95 masks in packs of ten for a reasonable price.[47]

To combat the second problem of effectiveness you can purchase a N-100 mask, though, they're quite expensive for a single mask simply because they're much better at filtering dust and debris. If interested, here's one N-100 mask option.[48]

There's also something to be said for how ineffective these masks are if you have facial hair like I do. Plus, to be truly effective they need to be properly fitted as not all masks correctly fit all faces right out of the box; picture a child wearing an adult-sized mask and you'll quickly understand what I mean.

Regardless, I'd suggest buying the ten pack of N-95 masks and including a few in each bug out bag. I've tried the N-100 rated masks and they're not quite as good as I'd hoped, at least, when price-compared to the N-95 rated masks.

I should briefly point out that there is NO reason to purchase something like a gas mask here. It will take up a lot of precious space in your bag and do no better in most cases than a typical N-95 mask for most scenarios you may encounter.

If interested, there's also the option of an RZ mask which I had the chance to review a while back if you'd prefer something that's even more durable and comfortable to wear.[49]

38. Chapstick / Vaseline

Both Chapstick and Vaseline have many uses for your survival, and there's no harm with including both of them in your bag since they take up very little space and add negligible weight. Either can be used to protect chapped lips, cover wounds, protect your face from windburn, and even as part of a makeshift fire starter. The Chapstick should also have a SPF protection rating.

If I had to pick one over the other, I would opt for the Vaseline. While you should be able to find relatively small bottles of it for sale, you could just take a spoonful or two and smear it inside a Ziploc bag or other small container if you wanted to save a bit of space in your bag. Granted, Vaseline will melt at around 100 degrees Fahrenheit, so package it well or you'll have a mess on your hands.

39. Duct Tape

Duct tape has so many uses that it's mind-boggling, and if you're a fan of the television show

Mythbusters, you know what I mean. Just be sure to purchase a quality name brand and avoid the knockoffs because if you need duct tape to stick then you really need it to stay in place. No doubt, during a bug out you'll want to ensure your duct tape repair stays put and doesn't fray or lose grip.

Odds are you probably don't need an entire roll since a full roll of tape can be heavy. As such, once you have one-third or less of a typical roll leftover from other uses, just smash the roll flat and toss it in your bag. Or, wrap several feet or more around an expired gift card; I do that and keep it in my wallet.

40. Solar Charging Kit

What's the plan when your gear dies, and your portable charger has run out of juice? Hopefully, you've made it to your destination by that time. If not, you're going to need a way to recharge it and about the only way I know of do that reliably is with a portable solar charging kit.

I know you may be getting tired of hearing this but since technology, size, capacity, and prices continue to change with portable solar chargers, I'm hesitant to offer a suggestion here, though, I have had the following Sunjack Portable Solar Charger for years and am quite happy with it.[50] I would suggest you search for *camping solar charger* online and you'll find plenty of options to choose from.

If interested, they also make solar-rechargeable portable USB chargers. They won't recharge their internal battery fast via solar powered, but they will eventually recharge if you're desperate. Ultimately, however, a solar charging kit of any kind is really only useful to keep your phone or tablet charged since everything that uses alkaline batteries can't be recharged with a typical solar-powered charger.

41. Anti-Chaffing Powder / Gel

If you're going to be walking quite a bit more than you're accustomed to, it's quite possible that sensitive spots on your body will chafe quickly, particularly where the legs rub together and armpits. Though you can use items like Vaseline or even cornstarch to help ease the pain, you may want to include a stick of anti-chaffing powder or gel like this Original Bodyglide, since it's made for this very purpose.[51]

42. Contractor Trash Bags

Suffice it to say that trash bags have many potential uses, for example, as an emergency rain poncho, water catch, or windbreak, to name a few. Be sure to purchase something like these large 42-gallon Husky Contractor Bags since they're bigger and significantly more sturdy than typical 13- or 32-gallon trash bags.[52] Add a few of these to each bug out bag you create.

Tier 4 Items: Your Needs May Require These

Now we're talking about items that may well not be needed in most cases yet could find use in very specific situations or for some people. Fortunately, many of these items are small and lightweight, so there's little reason not to include most of them, if possible.

43. Sunglasses

If you're overly sensitive to the sun, a pair of sunglasses may be a welcome addition to your bug out bag. And if you're going to add a pair, then you may as well get something that offers a bit of safety protection as well. I've used these Safety Sunglasses for years and, though they're no Ray-bans, they work quite well for the price.[53]

44. Disposable Camera

Why would you need a camera during an evacuation? A few reasons come to mind, such as to document anything you might encounter along your journey, for posterity, for use by law enforcement later if a crime has been committed, to document damages to your home or property, or merely to jog your memory.

Of course, so long as your smartphone is working then you can and should use that as a camera or video recorder since it will be better quality and you should be able to take many more photos than with a disposable camera. If you don't have a smartphone then consider including a disposable camera.

45. Deck of Cards

Compact and lightweight, card games are a great way to pass the time should you have some downtime or for when you get to your destination. Just grab any deck of cards at your local department store and toss them in.

46. E-Reader / Tablet

An e-reader or tablet is another potential way to pass the time, especially for kids who are accustomed to nonstop electronics. Be sure to load it up with plenty of books for you and games for the kids. Even better, download a wide variety of survival files for further reference. If you are going to add games, you'll want to know whether they require Wi-Fi to work or not and whether that's going to be a problem for you.

The good news is that you can get tablets cheap these days. As an example, I bought a Kindle Fire for a very reasonable price and, while it's not quite as good as even my old iPad, it will do the job as a bug out tablet.[54] Besides, it's relatively lightweight too.

Even though your smartphone should do in a pinch, you might also appreciate a larger screen to use for when you get to a safe bug out destination. And, since the tablet is yours, you won't have to worry about anyone stealing your personal information when you inevitably check your email or financials, for instance, at the local library or hotel business center.

47. Can Opener

If for some reason you packed cans of food without a pop top or purchased something along the way, then a can opener sure makes them easier to open. Don't bother with anything fancy, just buy a package of several P-38 or P-51 can openers.[55]

Add them to your bug out bag, vehicle kit, and keyring and you'll be sure to always have a relatively easy way to open canned foods at your disposal. Granted, these mini can openers won't open hundreds of cans, but they will get the job done during an evacuation.

48. Earplugs

I'm a light sleeper. For me earplugs are a must to include in my bags just so that I can sleep. Besides getting a better night's sleep, it's possible that things are merely noisy wherever you happen to be traveling. Earplugs are so small and lightweight it's easy to include a pair or two with your supplies and not even notice.

49. Super Siphon / Plastic Tubing

The Super Siphon is more useful, in my opinion, in a vehicle kit, though, it can also find use in your bug out bag to make transfer of water easier. To save space I would suggest that you include several feet of thin plastic tubing instead.

Why? Because a simple length of thin, clear plastic tubing can prove rather useful to retrieve water from a variety of otherwise inaccessible spots should the need ever arise. Just look at your local hardware or even an automotive store for what you need. Note: I'm told that surgical tubing works well for this purpose, though I've not tried it.

To store your tubing, simply coil it like you would cordage or an extension cord and try not to put too many kinks in it, though, one or two are likely inevitable.

50. Crowbar / Pry Bar

Crowbars. If you need one, then you probably need a really BIG one. The problem is that the big ones can get unnecessarily heavy for a bug out bag. Alternatively, a mini pry bar would be ideal in size and weight, but simply isn't big enough to be of any use. As such, we must compromise and opt for something in-between. This 15-inch Vaughan Superbar (or something similar) would be about the best that we can do to give you something useful, yet not overdo it on weight.[56]

Why would you need a pry bar besides breaking and entering, you ask? Of course, I'm not suggesting you use one for anything illicit whatsoever. But I will say that it's rather difficult to wrench open doors that may get stuck after a disaster with your bare hands.

51. Sillcock Key

Ever heard of a sillcock key? That's alright, I hadn't either until not too long ago. If you know anything about commercial building maintenance, however, you probably do.

You see, many commercial buildings don't have typical spigots like homes do. Instead, their outside water outlets are usually recessed and can only be turned on with an appropriate Sillcock Key which is very similar in design to a 4-way lug nut wrench, only a lot smaller.[57] I assume they do this to keep unauthorized people from accessing their water during normal times.

The good news is that some of these commercial buildings may still have accessible water but would otherwise be inaccessible without this special key. To be honest, I don't know how useful this item would truly be during an evacuation, but I figure that it's rather small to include, so why not?

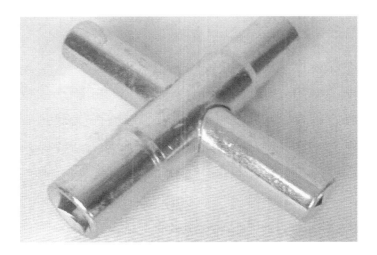

52. Vitamins

There's no reason not to give your body as many nutrients as you can during your bug out, especially since you're on the move and eating less than normal. While you can certainly forego vitamins since you're probably not going to be in a bad situation for months, there's no harm with having something extra, especially if you have young children.

53. Bible

Get a pocket Bible to comfort you and yours since emergencies are a time when many folks will be scared, nervous, and really need their faith more than ever. Though you can include Bible apps on your smartphone or tablet, there's no harm in also including a small pocket Bible too.

13 Items You Probably Don't Need

This final list of gear and supplies are probably not needed during a suburban bug out. I'm not saying you can't make use of them in some instances, but since we're trying to cut down on the amount of gear in your bag—and considering that we're not bugging out through the wilderness—you probably won't need any of the items listed here:

1. **Tent** – Unless you have a specific need, such as kids who prefer it over a tarp, most tents will take up too much space in your bag or merely weigh you down. That said, if you insist on a tent instead, then please do spend the money on a good quality backpacking tent so that it's lightweight, compact, and as durable as possible.

2. **Hammock** – I've recently become a fan of camping hammocks but, again, there's no reason to include one seeing as though there may not be any trees to attach it to.

3. **Sleeping Bag, Ground Pad** – Again, my vision for a suburban evacuation doesn't have you lying down and sleeping much. Nevertheless, if you see it differently, then you'll want an appropriate sleeping bag for the weather and a sleeping pad for both comfort and warmth.

4. **Cookset** – If you've taken my advice and opted for light snacks or MREs as your meal choice

then there's no point in any cooking gear whatsoever which also saves space.

5. **Portable Stove** – If you don't need the cookset then you won't need a stove either. That said, a stove could be useful for making water safe to consume, though, the LifeStraw does a great job and much faster too. Perhaps the only exception would be a viral outbreak.

6. **Signal Mirror** – I see little reason why you would need one in a suburban evacuation, especially since you're trying NOT to draw attention to yourself.

7. **Candles** – I'm not a fan of candles for lighting purposes in any situation and a bug out is no exception; they're just a fire hazard you don't need or want.

8. **Glow Sticks** – While glow sticks have a place in some bug out bag lists, there's no need to waste the space when the flashlights you've already included will work far better and for much longer.

9. **Fishing Kit** – I'd be shocked if somebody will ever make use of their fishing gear in a suburban bug out, and if you can then you're not evacuating through suburbia.

10. **Folding Shovel** – I almost wanted to include a shovel in my recommended items, and I wouldn't be opposed to doing so. That said, there may not be too many areas in a city where you'll be able to dig a hole for a

makeshift toilet and, besides, you probably won't be eating a whole lot anyway.

11. **Folding Saw, Pocket Chainsaw** — If you were expecting to start a fire then these items would come in handy. Of course, with a little know-how a fixed blade knife can easily perform any task that a pocket saw can.

12. **Snare Wire** — While there may very well be wild animals roaming your city, you won't have time to wait around to catch them.

13. **Sewing Kit** — I see no reason to have any sort of sewing kit in your bag. If you must repair a piece of clothing that is torn, for instance, use the duct tape. If you must have something else, then add a dozen or two large safety pins for expedient repairs.

I'm sure there are more wilderness-related gear that aren't needed in a suburban bag, though, the above list will get you started thinking about gear you may be tempted to include yet may not truly need.

After all, that's really what this chapter is about. Think about your family, where you live, what you might encounter, where you expect to go, and then decide which of the items I've recommended, too, that may not be truly useful to you either. And definitely think long and hard before adding any of the unnecessary items we just covered.

Evacuating by Vehicle

So, you've followed my advice and have your bug out bag supplies gathered, which is great! Now comes the hard part: putting together a plan to evacuate safely.

As you well know, most folks will prefer to bug out in a vehicle, opting only to do so by foot if they must. Your bug out bag is intended primarily for evacuating by foot, though, it could be of useful during a vehicle evacuation too. With that in mind, I would encourage you to have a plan to do both, but let's focus on evacuating using a vehicle first since that's what I expect your preference will be.

No doubt, evacuating in a vehicle has clear advantages, including being able to cover much more ground faster as well as the ability to take more gear and supplies with you, both of which are huge benefits in most scenarios. Realize that there are other benefits to using a vehicle such as being able to transport people who may have been injured or who are infirm, they offer more protection from inclement weather, and depending on the vehicle you choose you may have a self-sustainable environment, for instance, as with an RV or motorhome.

There are cons, too, such as a heavy reliance on roadways that may now be impassable, taking too long to evacuate because you're busy loading gear, as well as becoming a target if you're clearly one of the few vehicles still functional on the roads.

All things considered, I still plan on evacuating using a vehicle, if at all possible, and I suspect you will as well. Personally, since I currently have five people to care for along with our dog, trying to keep everyone moving for any length of time may be nearly impossible if we had to evacuate by foot. A vehicle makes a family evacuation easier on everyone, particularly me.

Specific Considerations for Vehicle Evacuation

To ensure your vehicle is as ready as possible for when the time comes, you really need to start now. Here's several crucial actions and concerns you need to understand now.

Perform a Dry Run

You might be surprised to find out that all of the extra gear and supplies you plan on taking with you simply won't fit in your car, especially after all of your family members and pets are included. Take some time to figure out precisely what you'll include, where it might fit, and what you simply cannot bring due to space restrictions. Pack wisely.

Only Take More Than One Vehicle if You Must

On the one hand, more than one vehicle means more ways that you can break down, get stuck, or run out of fuel. On the other hand, a second vehicle may offer you the ability to continue on if one car ceases to function. In my opinion, a second vehicle most likely means that you're just going to try and take more gear and supplies than you really should. Resist the urge.

Be Able to Take a Different Vehicle

I'll assume that one vehicle you own is preferred over the others because it may be more reliable, has off-road capabilities, or it can carry more supplies. Realize, however, that things do tend to go wrong when times are hardest. As such, you should have a plan to use an alternate vehicle should your primary choice be compromised. This may, therefore, necessitate a significant reduction in the supplies you can take. Prioritize your lists.

Consider Additional Cargo Carrier Options

If you feel like you simply MUST take more gear, there's an option for that, such as rooftop carriers, hitch-mounted cargo carriers, pull-behind utility trailers, truck bed camper shells and pop-tents, and more. Some ideas are more useful than others, but they will all limit your mobility to a degree. Consider utilizing these carefully before assuming they will work out well during a disaster scenario. Sometimes less really is more.

Always Keep Your Fuel Tank Half Full or More

I do this as a matter of practice in my daily life, and I encourage my family to do so also. After all, you never know if or when you may need to evacuate at a moment's notice or if you'll merely get stuck in traffic, and there's no telling if you'll be able to fill up before hitting the road. Running on empty as a matter of practice is just bad prepping. Moreover, if you can stockpile a few extra cans of gasoline to take with you then all the better.

Get Your Vehicle Ready for the Road

Ensure any routine vehicle maintenance is taken care of, that you have the ability to deal with problems you may encounter such as a flat tire or getting stuck in the mud, and that every licensed driver can actually drive the vehicle you expect to take. For instance, relying on a stick-shift vehicle when only you can drive one is probably a bad idea.

And if you want to be extra prepared, then it couldn't hurt to also include supplies that may be needed down the road if there's a problem, such as a tire repair kit, 12-volt air compressor, engine coolant, engine oil, serpentine belt, and the like.

List of Gear to Take

Make a list of the most important items you want to take along with their location in the house. I've actually made a three-tiered list of items that I want to take with me, separated into a 15-minute list, one-hour list, and one-day list, each one building upon the previous.

As an example, if I felt like I had to evacuate very quickly, I would focus on grabbing only the gear and supplies on my 15-minute list. This would include items like my family's bug out bags, extra gasoline, money, and firearms. Then, if I thought I had more time, I would grab items on my one-hour list, which includes extra food as well as some camping gear and clothing, to name a few examples. Finally, if I felt like I had significantly more time to pack then I would add other items on my one-day list.

In essence, **I'm going to grab the most crucial items first and work my way down the list as time permits**.

Here's an example of what I call a Priority Checklist that's included in one of my online survival courses which demonstrates the concept:

Priority Checklists

15 Minutes or Less

(Only the most basic items you will need to survive and get to safety)

Priority	Location	Item Description	Vehicle?	Got It?
High	Basement	Bug Out/G.O.O.D. Bags	SUV	
High	Garage	Stored Gasoline (in 5 gallon containers)	SUV	
Mod	Master Bedroom	Money (cash and coins)	SUV	
Mod	Master Closet	Firearms and Ammo	SUV	
Low	Utility Room	Pet Supplies (food, leash, collar, etc)	SUV	
High	Master Bath	Glasses/Contacts	SUV	
High	Kitchen	Prescription Medications	SUV	

1 Hour or Less

(More of what you can use - Items from the list above are assumed to be selected)

Priority	Location	Item Description	Vehicle?	Got It?
Mod	Garage	Camping Gear (tent, bags, stove, etc)	SUV	
Mod	Master Closet	Additional Clothes and Shoes (adults)	SUV	
Mod	Kids Closet	Additional Clothes and Shoes (children)	SUV	
High	Pantry	Pantry Foods (stored in sturdy totes)	SUV	
Low	Family Room	Cell Phone Chargers	SUV	
Mod	Hall Closet	Coats / Jackets (winter preps)	SUV	
Mod	Laundry Room	First Aid Supplies (and equipment)	SUV	

1 Day or Less

(Nice to have items if space and time permit - Items from the lists above are assumed to be selected)

Priority	Location	Item Description	Vehicle?	Got It?
Mod	Office	Collectibles (watches, jewelry, stamps, etc)	SUV	
High	Living Room	Laptop (including charger, case)	SUV	
Low	Garage	Toolbox	SUV	
Low	Storage Room	Extra Blankets / Bedding	SUV	
Mod	Master Closet	Firesafe Contents	SUV	

Again, it's just an example and not my actual list. In any case, there's more going on in that checklist example than I mentioned, such as a priority column for each of the three lists (high, medium, low), location of the item, as well as which vehicle it goes in if you're taking more than one car. Your list doesn't have to be quite that complex. In fact, a basic list of items separated into three levels of importance would suffice.

That said, I would encourage you to add a location for each item because you (1) may not be the one gathering these items and (2) regardless of what you may believe, everyone in the family may not know where these items are. Furthermore, disasters can be incredibly stressful and, as a result, you may not immediately remember where everything is yourself; a primer in the form of an easy-to-reference list can make your life just a bit easier when needed the most. I strongly encourage you to make one yourself.

What Type of Vehicle Should You Choose?

Spend any time on the Internet searching for bug out vehicles or, worse, on prepper forums, and you'll likely find a wide range of advice and opinions as to which vehicle is best for an apocalyptic-level evacuation.

Honestly, I wouldn't bother with trying to buy a vehicle specifically for this purpose or even with outfitting your current vehicle with anything tactical, such as push bumpers—like what police vehicles have—or armor plating. In most scenarios doing so is just a waste of money.

Now, I'm NOT saying that you shouldn't include items that may be of use, such as an electric winch for your

SUV or a cargo carrier, as mentioned previously. Just don't go overboard with outfitting your vehicle or get caught up in the hype of the Internet and you'll be fine.

Is it Even Possible to Evacuate in a Vehicle?

That might sound like a silly question, but it could be that roadways are impassable due to downed trees or power lines, road surfaces could be literally destroyed such as after an earthquake, or it could be that the roads are jam-packed with motorists all trying to evacuate themselves.

Whatever the reason, it's clear that evacuation in a vehicle may not be a viable option. At the very least, it may be that evacuating in the direction or along the roads you normally use may not be a viable option. That said, you may find that traveling in a completely different direction or via different roads is entirely possible, which is why it's crucial you plan your routes out now.

The Routes You Choose Matter Immensely

If you're relying on a vehicle, planning the routes you intend to use is probably the most important action you can take besides getting on the road as fast as possible. The problem is that you're likely going to choose the roadways you're most accustomed to driving which surely include the very same roadways everyone else will utilize, specifically highways and major city thoroughfares.

Unfortunately, you may not have a choice in the matter because there simply isn't a practical alternative. If you live in a major city, in particular, there may not be a viable, less-traveled roadway. In the suburbs you may have more leeway in finding navigable roads that others may not try or even be aware of, including neighborhoods, county or service roads, and even unpaved or off the map roads. Of course, I'm not suggesting that you willfully trespass on private or government-owned roadways, just that you should consider all possibilities when your very survival may be at stake.

In any case, this is where you really need to take some time to study your maps thoroughly. Open up your favorite maps program on the computer, use a map app on your phone, or grab a trusty paper map and take your time looking for less-traveled roads that will still get you to where you want to go, but aren't expected to be as busy.

Personally, I like to use Google Maps.[58] They have many useful features, including the ability to view satellite images, traffic estimates using typical traffic flow which shows how busy roads tend to be, street views, directions for walking, and plenty more. Take some time experimenting with the views and options and you'll surely find it useful as well. No matter which map option you use, planning your routes WILL take time and effort.

Now, I can't tell you which roads to take or precisely where to go. That's up to you to figure out based upon where you live and work, the time of day, where you're trying to evacuate to, as well as the extent of disaster. I can, however, say the following:

Include More Than One Destination

I know most of us tend to have ONE place in mind that we want to evacuate to above all others. That may be your bug out retreat, a family or friend's house in another state, or perhaps now's the time you're determined to get to Disneyland. It doesn't much matter, but you should have more than one place to go.

Even better, plan your bug out locations in each of the four cardinal directions: north, south, east, and west. If you cannot evacuate in each direction because you live on a peninsula, like I do, or for whatever reason, just do the best you can.

Avoid Busy Roadways Like the Plague

If you know certain roads are usually well-traveled during rush hour, then these are roads that should be avoided whenever possible because they're the very same roadways everyone else will naturally be trying to use during an evacuation. I will almost guarantee that they will be even worse than normal during an emergency situation. If you cannot avoid traveling on these busy roads, then you really need to get moving immediately.

Plan Multiple Routes to Each Location

This is where planning begins to get tedious. If you'll make the effort, attempt to plan multiple routes to each bug out location identified and be ready and willing to deviate from those routes, if necessary.

Even if you must deviate at some point, at least you have an initial route planned to begin with along with an alternative to fall back on. Local paper maps are good to keep in each vehicle for this very reason, plus you won't have to remember to grab them before evacuating.

In addition, having an offline maps app for your phone may be of use too. As such, I would encourage each adult in your family to have an offline maps app with appropriate local and state maps already downloaded; I've been using Offline Maps & Navigation, though, there are other options.[59]

Plan Both Long-Distance and Local Bug Out Destinations

Long-distance destinations should be maybe one or two hundred miles at most, usually nothing more than a single tank of gas. Local destinations could simply be the next town over but shouldn't merely be your neighbor's house.

You'll quickly find that this is where bug out planning gets downright tiresome because you'll quickly find that you have so many routes going that it can get confusing quickly. Fortunately, it's likely that most long-distance destinations will utilize a portion of the same routes that closer bug out locations do which will help.

In any case, I suggest you print out complete directions for all destinations and include them in a bug out binder, your bug out bags, or already in your vehicle.

Fuel and Time Factors Will Increase

You're probably going to use more fuel and take much more time than you otherwise would to get to where you're going, perhaps much more than you realize. This is one more reason why it's imperative that you keep your gas tank half full or more at all times and also why I suggest you bring extra, full cans of gas during your evacuation too.

Warning: Do not place cans of can in the passenger compartment of any vehicle since evaporating fumes will make you sick. They must be secured to the outside of your vehicle for your safety.

Compile Names, Addresses, and Phone Numbers

Even after you've identified several bug out destinations, both near and far, I'll assume that some of those are going to require you to rent a hotel or motel room once you get there. To save yourself time and to beat others to it you should have a list of places to stay already compiled, including the name of the place, their address, and phone number. I would suggest you have three options listed, though more won't hurt. Most of the time you can do a simple online search and print this information out relatively quickly.

The key points to remember when using a vehicle for evacuation are these:

- Make a list of the important items you want to take. Your bug out bag is a great start, but still make a list of everything crucial to your survival so you're ready-to-go.
- Perform a dry run beforehand so that you know what fits and be able to use another vehicle, if you must, which may necessitate you taking fewer supplies.
- Plan your bug out locations and routes thoroughly now. Take your time, print directions out, and share your plans with others in the family. I would encourage you to keep these plans in your vehicles, so you don't have to remember to grab them later.

- You won't get far without fuel. Be sure to always keep your vehicle gas tank half full, stockpile extra cans of fuel properly treated with fuel stabilizer and rotate the stored gasoline at least once a year to ensure freshness.
- Get on the road ASAP. It won't matter what you choose to take with you or how well you packed if you're stuck in traffic and must now continue by foot.

Evacuating by Foot

If you're to the point where you must evacuate by foot, that's not good. Even though you're going to be better prepared because you have a backpack full of gear and supplies, let's review three assumptions I'm willing to make about your status:

1. **You can't evacuate in a vehicle**, otherwise you probably would have which means you're going to spend more time in a potentially dangerous area due to widespread devastation of buildings and infrastructure. It could, for instance, take you days to evacuate if you must walk around and climb over piles of rubble or if you must go completely out of your way due to something as simple as an impassable bridge.
2. **You'll have less supplies to rely upon** because you likely would have chosen to take extra food and water if evacuating in a vehicle, most people would. This, therefore, leaves you more vulnerable if you're unable to get to safety in a timely manner by foot.
3. **You're going to be in close proximity to many more unprepared people** in a suburban or urban environment than, say, during a wilderness bug out. As such, if you and your family clearly look more prepared than

everyone else then you could easily become a target of their desperation.

The good news is that everyone else will initially be dazed by the disaster and confused about what to do, still reeling from what just happened, and not yet looking at you as a target. This is your window of opportunity, and because you have a plan in place, you'll be fast on your way out of the danger area before anyone realizes it.

This is why it's crucial that you (1) have the gear and supplies already gathered so you can get moving immediately and (2) know where to go and how you'll get there so there's no guessing or confusion on your part.

The bug out bag you just created takes care of gathering the supplies you need which means you can get moving immediately. Similar to evacuating in a vehicle, planning the routes you will use to bug out will take care of knowing where you'll go and how you'll get there. Of course, the routes you plan to use could change drastically if there is widespread damage to buildings and roadways. In fact, what were once well-known areas of the city to you may look unrecognizable after a disaster strikes. Even so, it's still good to have an initial plan to rely upon.

With that in mind, plan out your evacuation locations and routes just as you would if using a vehicle to evacuate. That is, use your favorite map program, print out the directions, and keep them with your bug out bag. Before stashing your plans away, be sure to discuss locations and routes with other family members so they know what to do.

How Far Should You Expect to Walk?

That's tough to answer as it largely depends on the severity and type of disaster you encounter. An earthquake, for instance, could devastate many square miles and necessitate a much longer walk to safety than a tornado might, whereas a hurricane could effectively wreck multiple neighboring states at once. Don't expect to be walking hundreds of miles no matter what you're facing. One or two dozen miles over the course of a day or two is more realistic.

Should You Follow Roadways or Not?

Everyone knows that the shortest distance between two points is a straight line, so it should stand to reason that you ought to walk directly to your bug out location, even if that's over the hills and through the trees, right? Not so fast.

The problem is that, depending on where you live, such terrain may be much more difficult to traverse thereby delaying your evacuation more so than spending the extra time to follow already established roadways. For example, where I live there are plenty of trees and patches of forest that we could choose to walk through, yet thick vegetation, steep hills, and unstable terrain may slow us down more than it would benefit us.

On the other hand, you may find that some roadways are simply impassable after disaster, all but forcing you to occasionally traverse unpaved terrain. In addition, it may be significantly safer to avoid roadways as the aftermath continues and people become increasingly desperate.

So, what's the right answer? It depends on many factors, such as how bad the disaster is, the terrain where you live, your physical ability, as well as how much time has elapsed. If I had to give an answer then I'd say stick to the paved roadways as much as possible early on, say, during the first twenty-four hours; only move to the woods if you're forced to or if you're still walking a day or two after and it's clear others' desperation has begun to set in.

What if a Family Member is Not Home?

My expectation when creating your bug out plans is that you're starting from home. For some this isn't always going to be the case, especially for those who work elsewhere for a living. As such, you generally have two choices:

1. Create an entirely new set of evacuation plans starting from your place of employment or any other significant place you frequent and include those in your bag as well.
2. Expect that you'll return home first and start your evacuation from there or, if you must, pick a meet-up point for all family members to rally before continuing on.

Choosing option one will surely allow you to get out of the danger area faster, but it potentially leaves you guessing as to whether or not your family members were able to evacuate safely too, particularly if you're unable to communicate with them in the moment. After all, you cannot and should not expect that phone lines will be functional after a disaster. That said, text messages are more likely to get through than phone calls during an emergency situation. Even so, there's no guarantee that a text message will be delivered in a timely manner either.

Choosing option two clearly means you're going to take longer to get out of the danger area, possibly to your detriment, but it also means that you and your family will attempt the majority of their evacuation together, plus you'll be more able to keep them safe if everyone is together.

Personally, I would almost always choose to gather my family. Perhaps the only time I might choose not to is if one family member worked a long distance away such that it made returning home first pointless. Even then I would still want to communicate with them via phone or a text message beforehand to ensure everyone is on the same page. Ultimately, you're at the mercy of communication infrastructure and, more importantly, how well you planned for just such a scenario.

My advice would be to choose one of the following:

1. If you and your family tend to work or travel relatively close to home, then use that as your starting point and instruct all family members to return home before evacuating.
2. If one or more people work or travel a significant distance away during the day, then choose an acceptable meet-up location so you can evacuate together.

What if You Can't Call or Text After a Disaster?

You should work on the assumption that you cannot communicate after disaster. Doing so will force you and your family to determine what happens if your initial plans don't go as expected.

That is, if your plan is to return home and evacuate together, what will you do if not everyone shows up within a set timeframe, say, twenty-four hours? Will you wait another day and then leave, evacuate to a predetermined bug out destination no matter what, or go straight to a meet-up spot? Which bug out destination takes priority and how will others know if locations change? Who gets to make those decisions if you're the one who didn't return home?

The only way to know is to have these questions answered beforehand.

How Far to Take Your Plans?

Evacuation planning can get far more complicated than what I've discussed thus far, such as by having more than one meet-up location depending which family member is where at the time, prioritizing bug out locations or routes depending on where the disaster strikes (e.g., the epicenter of an earthquake could necessitate evacuating to an alternate destination), using pre-determined texts and responses to enact specific plans, and more.

Truth be told, that's a bit more effort than even I am willing to give my plans. We do have specific bug out locations picked out, routes to take, and places to stay identified. If you can do those three things, then you'll be well ahead of almost everyone else.

Three Additional Concerns Regarding on Foot Evacuation

As if what we've covered thus far wasn't enough, there are three more problems you need to be aware of so that you can manage them properly.

You'll Cover Much Less Distance Than You Expect

The average walking speed is roughly three miles per hour, give or take a bit depending on your height and gait. Factor in the terrain, possibly having to take alternate routes or even backtracking, your party's overall fitness, the fact that you're lugging around a relatively heavy backpack, much-needed rest breaks, as well as how fast others in your party may be able to move, and I'd be surprised if you travel much more than a mile per hour during most of your bug out. Maybe you'll start off at a good pace because of all the adrenaline but expect that to diminish quickly as the hours pass by.

Because of this, you really shouldn't expect to travel much more than a dozen miles in a day, all things considered. Granted, that's merely a generalization; your distance traveled may vary considerably and only you can attempt to determine how far you and your family may be able to travel in a single day. I would suggest that you plan for a conservative number and be happy if you get further.

Inability to Carry Gear

Another problem some folks may have is that they're unable to carry a backpack of any size due to having a bad back or knees, even if it's relatively lightweight. If this applies to you then you can choose to either have another family member pack some supplies for you or attempt to utilize a rolling suitcase or something like it that you can pull yourself. Both have drawbacks, particularly having to rely on someone else who may not be around during an evacuation. Only you and your family can determine which idea will work best. Perhaps you should have the ability to do both.

You might also consider caching some supplies at your bug out locations or even strategically along routes. This could be a useful idea no matter whether you're capable of carrying your own gear or not, but it could also leave you susceptible until you can get to your supplies. Moreover, cached supplies could also become damaged or stolen without you knowing until it's too late. Because of this, I really wouldn't bother with attempting to cache supplies unless you have one specific place in mind, such as a bug out cabin in the woods.

The Target on Your Back

This is probably what worries me the most during an evacuation, more so than running out of fuel or food and even more than freezing to death, because a large hiking backpack screams out that I have stuff to the unprepared and desperate masses. Regrettably, there really isn't a perfect solution to this problem. That is, you either take a chance and have supplies with you or risk your very survival by taking much less.

One solution could be to minimize how much you stand out, yet still have something to rely upon, such as with a Get Home Bag, though you will have less gear to rely upon and still possibly become a target simply because you appear to have something others may need.[60]

Personally, I'd rather have more supplies than I may need to survive and to deal with confrontations if I must, but you may not.

Concluding Thoughts Regarding Evacuation Planning

Evacuation planning is nothing to gloss over. Sure, having a bug out bag and the supplies to see you through is a great start, but not having a proper plan can be almost as disastrous as not having the right gear.

Go ahead and begin making of list of the more important items you expect to take in a vehicle, besides your bug out bags. This shouldn't take long and will likely include items such as:

- Money, important documents, memorabilia, collectibles, or family heirlooms
- Additional clothing, jackets, shoes
- Extra supplies (water, food, prescription medications, fuel, phone chargers, etc.)
- Firearms and ammunition
- Camping gear (tent, sleeping bags, camping stoves, etc.)
- Laptop or other electronics
- Extra pet supplies (food, leash, toys, etc.)

Next, consider which vehicle is your best option and, as I've mentioned before, perform a dry run to figure out what can really fit. If you insist on using a cargo carrier or a trailer, for example, then do whatever you can now to make is as easy as possible to attach and get on the move ASAP. That is, you could permanently install a rooftop cargo carrier now or pre-position a trailer so it's more easily accessible and ready to be hitched.

Once you've got your list together, take an hour and plan your escape. At the very least, pick out good bug out locations, both near and far, as well as places you can stay when you get there. If that's going to be a motel or hotel then gather addresses and phone numbers for each of them. If it's a friend or family member then be sure they're aware of and receptive to your intentions to come to their house.

Last, you need to figure out how to get to each of your bug out locations which, as you'll quickly realize, is easier said than done. Try to avoid the more trafficked roadways and trouble spots you'll likely encounter or drive a portion of a route, even during rush hour, to determine what type of traffic you might encounter and where you might be able to deviate. When finished, print out your directions and include them in your vehicle and bug out bags.

Remember that a few hours of planning now could alleviate a ton of trouble later. There's also no harm in reevaluating your plans periodically just in case something changes. I do this once a year. You'll definitely want to make changes when major events occur, such as moving homes, changing jobs, or you stopped talking to your brother-in-law and now you're no longer welcome there.

Last, as I stated earlier, I've included several worksheets you can make use of or simply use as a thought-starter to better enact your bug out plans. I've added a checklist of gear and supplies, evacuation procedures and directions, as well as contacts that you may want to include in your bug out bags. You can find these worksheets in the appendices or you may download a PDF format of them for free here: https://rethinksurvival.com/books/plans.html.[61]

The Suburban Bug Out Bag Recap

We've covered a lot of ground in this book. Yes, we've intentionally left out some items, most of which are probably unnecessary in a suburban bug out bag, but we did include 53 essentials that can and should be included in your bag in most cases.

Of course, I'm sure some folks will take issue with the relative placement of various items—the fixed blade knife showing up in tier three comes to mind—but please don't let any of that stop you from taking my overall advice since you're free to move items around as you see fit.

Remember that the purpose of this bag isn't to keep you well fed and warm in the wilderness for a week or two. Rather, it's intended to get you from point A to point B as quickly and as safely as possible in a suburban environment with considerably different requirements than most wilderness scenarios.

Though divided into tiers, I really feel that every item listed here is worthy of being included in your bag. That said, if you must focus your money and efforts on less gear then go for tier one and tier two items to start with. Add tiers three and four gear and supplies when you can.

Remember, too, that some supplies need to be checked on and replaced regularly, including food and water, medications (especially prescriptions) and first aid items, hygiene supplies, and batteries, to name the most important ones. You'll also want to check on your clothing yearly and generally look everything over just to ensure nothing was damaged somehow.

When you're all said and done, and assuming you've taken my advice, your bag should weigh under thirty pounds. Mine weighs about twenty-eight pounds as of this writing, and my wife's bag weighs a pound or two less than that. If you want to add more gear, you can, but be careful about going overboard here since you'll want to stay light on your feet.

Understand, too, that creating a bug out bag is only half the battle. You really do need to take the time now to figure out a solid evacuation plan. Yes, it will take both time and effort on your part, but it will be time well spent should you ever actually need to evacuate.

Now, go grab yourself a good quality hiking bag and stuff it full of the gear discussed previously. You'll be more prepared than 99% of the folks out there who have failed to do anything and ready to tackle a disaster head-on.

Get Your Free Checklist Here

Before you grab your checklist, be a good friend or family member and choose to help others who could use this crucial information.

Spread the Word, Share the Knowledge

I'm willing to bet that you have family and friends who could benefit from this book as well, so please take a moment right now and quickly share a link to it on Facebook, Twitter, or Pinterest. You can easily do so here.[62]

Now, download your free, easy-to-reference 53-point suburban bug out bag checklist here.[63] Or, if you prefer, the entire checklist is reproduced in Appendix A for your convenience.

Discover More Survival Books Here

If you liked what you read within then you're going to love my other survival books.[64] Here's a sampling:

- 47 Easy DIY Survival Projects[65]
- The Complete Pet Safety Action Plan[66]
- 28 Powerful Home Security[67]
- 27 Crucial Smartphone Apps for Survival[68]
- 57 Scientifically-Proven Survival Foods to Stockpile[69]
- 75 of the Best Secret Hiding Places[70]
- Your Identity Theft Protection Game Plan[71]
- 144 Survival Uses for 10 Common Items[72]
- The Get Home Bag and Compact EDC Kit[73]

Recommended for You...

I want to point out one book from the above list, in particular, since you now clearly recognize the importance of being prepared while on the go: *27 Crucial Smartphone Apps for Survival: How to Use Free Phone Apps to Unleash Your Most Important Survival Tool*.

Did You Know You Have One of THE Most Powerful Survival Tools Already in Your Pocket?

That's right, the very same smartphone with dozens of mobile apps which most of us only use to play games, watch videos, and endlessly surf social media is a crucial tool for your survival IF you know what to do with it… and it's just waiting to be unleashed.

This book is designed to quickly show YOU how to turn your smartphone into a powerhouse tool that few people take advantage of.

We'll cover more than two dozen smartphone apps that you really must have, including emergency alert apps to keep you well-informed both before and after disaster strikes, navigational apps to keep you on track even when GPS is down, first aid apps to keep you healthy and safe, as well as several more crucial apps you may not have even considered… all of which could just save your life.

Discover precisely how to unleash your most important survival tool today.[74]

Your Opinion Matters to Me

I'd love to hear your feedback about this book, especially anything I might be able to add or improve upon for future revisions. Please send an email to rethinksurvival@gmail.com with the word "book" in the subject if you have something for me. (And be sure to include the book title so I'm not confused.)

Review This Book on Amazon

Last, I ask that you take a moment and write a review of my book on Amazon.com so that others know what to expect, particularly if you've found my advice useful.[75]

I do hope that you've enjoyed this book and that you will choose to implement my recommendations to help you and your family stay safe from disasters of all kinds, big or small.

I encourage you to please take a moment and download the 53-point checklist above, share this book with your friends and family using the link I provided previously, and leave a quick review on Amazon.com while you're at it.

May God bless you and your family.

Thank you for your time, Damian

Appendices

Appendix A: 53-Point Checklist

Appendix B: Priority Checklist

Appendix C: Evacuation Procedures

Appendix D: Evacuation Directions

Appendix E: Emergency Contacts

Appendix F: List of Resources

Appendix A: 53-Point Checklist

The following is sorted in alphabetical order by tiers; create one bag for each family member:

TIER 1 GEAR AND SUPPLIES

- Bug Out Plan, Information
- Cash, Small Bills ($20 bills or smaller)
- Change of Clothes, Shoes
- Extra Glasses/Contacts, Hearing Aid Batteries
- First Aid Supplies
- Flashlights, Headlamp (plus extra batteries)
- Local Maps, Destination Maps
- OTC Medications, Prescription Pills
- Pocket AM/FM/SW Radio
- Portable Phone Charger, Extra Cords
- Quick Foods, Snacks, Hard Candies
- Self Defense Option(s)
- Ultralight Tarp, Stakes, Guyline Tensioners
- Water Bottle/Canteen, Stainless Steel
- Water Filtration Option
- Weatherproof Jacket, Rain Poncho

TIER 2 GEAR AND SUPPLIES

- AMK Heatsheets / Bivvy
- Binoculars / Monocular
- Compass
- Cordage, Wire Ties, or Straps
- FRS/GMRS Radios

- Hat, Bandannas
- Hygiene Supplies
- Insect Repellent/Mosquito Head Net
- MREs (not freeze-dried meals)
- Multi-tool
- Spork (if meals are included)
- Sunblock
- Trauma Dressings
- Wet Wipes, Toilet Paper
- Work Gloves/Nitrile Gloves

TIER 3 GEAR AND SUPPLIES

- Anti-Chaffing Powder/Gel
- Chapstick, Vaseline
- Collapsible Water Bottle
- Contractor Trash Bags
- Duct Tape
- Fire Starters, Tinder
- Fixed-Blade Knife
- N-95 Masks
- Notepad and Pencil
- Solar Charging Kit
- Whistle

Whistle TIER 4 GEAR AND SUPPLIES

- Bible
- Can Opener
- Crowbar/Pry Bar
- Deck of Cards

- Disposable Camera
- Earplugs
- E-Reader/Tablet
- Sillcock (4-way) Key
- Sunglasses
- Super Siphon/Plastic Tubing
- Vitamins

Additional gear or supplies you want to include:

_____

_____

_____

_____

_____

_____

_____

_____

_____

Appendix B: Priority Checklist

15 Minutes or Less

Item Description	Location	Have It?
_____	_____	Yes / No
_____	_____	Yes / No
_____	_____	Yes / No
_____	_____	Yes / No
_____	_____	Yes / No
_____	_____	Yes / No

One Hour or Less

Item Description	Location	Have It?
_____	_____	Yes / No
_____	_____	Yes / No
_____	_____	Yes / No
_____	_____	Yes / No
_____	_____	Yes / No
_____	_____	Yes / No

One Day or Less

Item Description	Location	Have It?
_____	_____	Yes / No
_____	_____	Yes / No
_____	_____	Yes / No
_____	_____	Yes / No
_____	_____	Yes / No
_____	_____	Yes / No

Appendix C: Evacuation Procedures

The Decision to Leave

Chain of Command:

Who in the family says if we evacuate or not, regardless of what anyone else thinks? If that person is absent, who's the next two people in charge?

- 1st in charge: _____
- 2nd in charge: _____
- 3rd in charge: _____

How is the Decision to Evacuate Made? (If evacuation orders have been given, follow them.)

Does it depend on the type of disaster, expected length of the aftermath, or only on whether your home is still a viable shelter?

_____
_____
_____
_____

How are Special Circumstances Planned For?

That is, what if a family member has known mobility issues or health concerns? What about kids and pets?

_____
_____
_____
_____

What's the Plan if Family Members Are Away?

Are you going to expect everyone to regroup at home first or meet-up somewhere instead? Does type of disaster, time of day, or ability to contact one another immediately afterward make a difference?

_____

_____

_____

_____

Rendezvous / Meet-Up Procedures

General Procedures Regarding Your Meet-Up Location

Will you have more than one meet-up location? If so, how will everyone know where to go? Is there a safe place to wait until all family members arrives?

_____

_____

_____

_____

Procedures if Time is Exceeded and Some are Waiting?

What's the timeframe for moving on if someone doesn't show up? For those who didn't arrive on time, what's their next plan of action?

_____

_____

_____

_____

Appendix D: Evacuation Directions

Cardinal Direction (circle one): North / South / East / West

Repeat this worksheet for each of the four cardinal directions, if possible.

Local Destination (usually no more than a few dozen miles walking distance)

Full Address (or list only the nearby City and State):

_____

Primary Route: _____

Secondary Route: _____

Local Hotels (good to include even if you expect to stay with family or friends):

Name: _____ Phone: _____
Address: _____

Name: _____ Phone: _____
Address: _____

Out-of-Area Destination (usually no more than one or two hundred miles drive by vehicle)

Full Address (or list only the City and State):

_____

Primary Route: _____

Secondary Route: _____

Out-of-Area Hotels (always include even if you expect to stay with family or friends):

Name: _____ Phone: _____
Address: _____

Name: _____ Phone: _____
Address: _____

Name: _____ Phone: _____
Address: _____

Name: _____ Phone: _____
Address: _____

Meet-Up Location, if applicable

Primary Address (or general description of area):

_____

Alternate Address (or general description of area):

_____

Appendix E: Emergency Contacts

Examples: electricity, water, natural gas, phone.

Type	Provider Name	Phone Number
_____	_____	_____
_____	_____	_____
_____	_____	_____
_____	_____	_____
_____	_____	_____

Insurance Contacts

Examples: home, rental, auto, business, medical.

Type	Provider Name	Phone Number
_____	_____	_____
_____	_____	_____
_____	_____	_____
_____	_____	_____
_____	_____	_____

Financial Contacts

Examples: bank accounts, brokerage, 401K, IRA.

Type	Provider Name	Phone Number
_____	_____	_____
_____	_____	_____
_____	_____	_____
_____	_____	_____
_____	_____	_____
_____	_____	_____

Professional Contacts

Examples: doctor, pharmacist, accountant, attorney, financial planner, tax advisor.

Type	Provider Name	Phone Number
_____	_____	_____
_____	_____	_____
_____	_____	_____
_____	_____	_____
_____	_____	_____

Recover Services Contacts

Examples: fire/flood recovery, tree limb removal, electrician, plumber, general contractor.

Type	Provider Name	Phone Number
_____	_____	_____
_____	_____	_____
_____	_____	_____
_____	_____	_____
_____	_____	_____

Appendix F: List of Resources

- Link 1: https://rethinksurvival.com/books/bug-out-bag-checklist.php
- Link 2: https:// rethinksurvival.com/books/bag-book-offer.php
- Link 3: https://rethinksurvival.com/kindle-books/
- Link 4: https://rethinksurvival.com/kindle-books/bug-out-bag-recommends/#wagon
- Link 5: https://besthiking.net/hiking-backpacks-guide/
- Link 6: https://rethinksurvival.com/kindle-books/bug-out-bag-recommends/#backpack
- Link 7: https://rethinksurvival.com/books/get-12-pillars-of-survival.php
- Link 8: https://rethinksurvival.com/books/plans.html
- Link 9: http://graywolfsurvival.com/1014/how-to-plan-bugout-route/
- Link 10: https://rethinksurvival.com/kindle-books/bug-out-bag-recommends/#poncho
- Link 11: https://rethinksurvival.com/kindle-books/bug-out-bag-recommends/#bottle
- Link 12: https://rethinksurvival.com/how-to-purify-water-with-more-concentrated-bleach/
- Link 13: https://rethinksurvival.com/kindle-books/bug-out-bag-recommends/#potable
- Link 14: https://rethinksurvival.com/kindle-books/bug-out-bag-recommends/#lifestraw
- Link 15: https://rethinksurvival.com/kindle-books/bug-out-bag-recommends/#datrex

- Link 16: https://rethinksurvival.com/kindle-books/bug-out-bag-recommends/#mainstay
- Link 17: https://rethinksurvival.com/kindle-books/bug-out-bag-recommends/#maglite
- Link 18: https://rethinksurvival.com/kindle-books/bug-out-bag-recommends/#cree
- Link 19: https://rethinksurvival.com/kindle-books/smartphone-survival-apps-book/
- Link 20: https://rethinksurvival.com/kindle-books/bug-out-bag-recommends/#charger
- Link 21: https://rethinksurvival.com/kindle-books/bug-out-bag-recommends/#amfmradio
- Link 22: http://www.theradiosource.com/resources/stations-alert.htm
- Link 23: https://rethinksurvival.com/kindle-books/bug-out-bag-recommends/#tarp
- Link 24: https://rethinksurvival.com/kindle-books/bug-out-bag-recommends/#travelbag
- Link 25: https://rethinksurvival.com/kindle-books/bug-out-bag-recommends/#bandanna
- Link 26: https://rethinksurvival.com/kindle-books/bug-out-bag-recommends/#gloves
- Link 27: https://rethinksurvival.com/kindle-books/bug-out-bag-recommends/#heatsheets
- Link 28: https://rethinksurvival.com/kindle-books/bug-out-bag-recommends/#blanket
- Link 29: https://rethinksurvival.com/kindle-books/bug-out-bag-recommends/#bivvy
- Link 30: https://rethinksurvival.com/kindle-books/bug-out-bag-recommends/#spork

- Link 31: https://rethinksurvival.com/kindle-books/bug-out-bag-recommends/#binoculars
- Link 32: https://rethinksurvival.com/kindle-books/bug-out-bag-recommends/#leatherman
- Link 33: https://rethinksurvival.com/kindle-books/bug-out-bag-recommends/#radio
- Link 34: https://rethinksurvival.com/kindle-books/bug-out-bag-recommends/#bandage
- Link 35: https://www.youtube.com/watch?v=Z-UreiTgvHY
- Link 36: https://rethinksurvival.com/kindle-books/bug-out-bag-recommends/#paracord
- Link 37: https://rethinksurvival.com/kindle-books/bug-out-bag-recommends/#spooltool
- Link 38: https://rethinksurvival.com/kindle-books/bug-out-bag-recommends/#coldsteel
- Link 39: https://rethinksurvival.com/kindle-books/bug-out-bag-recommends/#gerbergator
- Link 40: https://rethinksurvival.com/kindle-books/bug-out-bag-recommends/#notebook
- Link 41: https://rethinksurvival.com/kindle-books/bug-out-bag-recommends/#pen
- Link 42: https://rethinksurvival.com/kindle-books/bug-out-bag-recommends/#vapur
- Link 43: https://rethinksurvival.com/kindle-books/bug-out-bag-recommends/#whistle
- Link 44: https://rethinksurvival.com/kindle-books/bug-out-bag-recommends/#firesteel
- Link 45: https://rethinksurvival.com/kindle-books/bug-out-bag-recommends/#tinder

- Link 46: https://www.doh.wa.gov/Portals/1/Documents/Pubs/334-353.pdf
- Link 47: https://rethinksurvival.com/kindle-books/bug-out-bag-recommends/#masks
- Link 48: https://rethinksurvival.com/kindle-books/bug-out-bag-recommends/#n100
- Link 49: https://rethinksurvival.com/rz-mask/
- Link 50: https://rethinksurvival.com/kindle-books/bug-out-bag-recommends/#solarcharger
- Link 51: https://rethinksurvival.com/kindle-books/bug-out-bag-recommends/#bodyglide
- Link 52: https://rethinksurvival.com/kindle-books/bug-out-bag-recommends/#trashbags
- Link 53: https://rethinksurvival.com/kindle-books/bug-out-bag-recommends/#sunglasses
- Link 54: https://rethinksurvival.com/kindle-books/bug-out-bag-recommends/#kindle
- Link 55: https://rethinksurvival.com/kindle-books/bug-out-bag-recommends/#canopener
- Link 56: https://rethinksurvival.com/kindle-books/bug-out-bag-recommends/#prybar
- Link 57: https://rethinksurvival.com/kindle-books/bug-out-bag-recommends/#sillcock
- Link 58: https://www.google.com/maps
- Link 59: https://play.google.com/store/apps/details?id=com.navigation.offlinemaps.gps&hl=en_US
- Link 60: https://rethinksurvival.com/kindle-books/get-home-bag-book/
- Link 61: https://rethinksurvival.com/books/plans.html

- Link 62: https://rethinksurvival.com/books/bug-out-bag-share-v2.html
- Link 63: https://rethinksurvival.com/books/bug-out-bag-checklist.php
- Link 64: https://rethinksurvival.com/kindle-books/
- Link 65: https://rethinksurvival.com/kindle-books/diy-survival-projects-book/
- Link 66: https://rethinksurvival.com/kindle-books/pet-safety-plan-book/
- Link 67: https://rethinksurvival.com/kindle-books/home-security-book/
- Link 68: https://rethinksurvival.com/kindle-books/smartphone-survival-apps-book/
- Link 69: https://rethinksurvival.com/kindle-books/survival-foods-book/
- Link 70: https://rethinksurvival.com/kindle-books/secret-hides-book/
- Link 71: https://rethinksurvival.com/kindle-books/id-theft-book/
- Link 72: https://rethinksurvival.com/kindle-books/survival-uses-book/
- Link 73: https://rethinksurvival.com/kindle-books/get-home-bag-book/
- Link 74: https://rethinksurvival.com/kindle-books/smartphone-survival-apps-book/
- Link 75: https://rethinksurvival.com/books/bug-out-bag-review-v2.php

Made in the USA
Columbia, SC
18 May 2020